TEXTBOOK OF

PHARMACEUTICAL ANALYSIS

Concepts on Titrimetric Analysis Done in Pharmacy

TEXTBOOK OF PHARMACEUTICAL ANALYSIS

Concepts on Titrimetric Analysis Done in Pharmacy

Subarna Ganguli
M.Pharma
Assistant Prof., Calcutta Institute of Pharmaceutical Technology and Allied Health Sciences, Banitabla, Uluberia, Howrah, West Bengal

AITBS PUBLISHERS, INDIA
MEDICAL PUBLISHERS
J-5/6, Krishan Nagar, Delhi-110051 (INDIA)
Phone: 011-40167052, 49067602; Fax: 011-22009074
E-mail: aitbsindia@gmail.com & aitbsindia@hotmail.com

First Edition: 2011
Second Edition: 2025

ISBN: 978-93-7473-484-1

Published by:
Virender Kumar Arya for
AITBS Publishers, India
MEDICAL PUBLISHERS
J-5/6, Krishan Nagar, Delhi-110051 (INDIA)
Phone: 011-40167052, 49067602; Fax: 011-22009074
E-mail: aitbsindia@gmail.com & aitbsindia@hotmail.com

Printed by AITBS, Delhi

This Book is Dedicated to

My Parents

PREFACE

This book is useful to students of Diploma, Degree and Post-Graduate level. Though several books are available in Analytical Chemistry but they are of high technical standard and students are not in position to follow them properly. This book is written in such a way so that students will be able to grasp the different methods of titrations adopted to assay several drugs and pharmaceuticals.

In addition to theoretical aspects, this book provides practical aspects too, which will help for students to perform practicals in laboratory. All practical procedures with principle and suitable examples are provided in very easy way.

Chapter 9 concentrates with estimation of functional groups present in a compound. Students will be gainer because it provides calculations along with procedures.

Chapter 10 deals with illustrative examples of Assay of Pharmaceutical Substances which are done by titrimetric methods. This chapter is totally practical oriented. Titrimetric methods, i.e., acidimetry and alkalimetry, oxidation-reduction titration, precipitation titration, complexometric titration, gravimetric analysis and non-aqueous titration are discussed with procedures, calculations for better understanding of students in practical classes.

I am sure this book will provide better understanding of Analytical Chemistry to the students of Pharmacy and Chemistry. It is my sincere request to offer critical comments and suggests from all levels.

We are also thankful to Virender Kumar Arya and his team at AITBS Publishers, Delhi, for their meticulous efforts in the direction of bringing out this book on time.

– Subarna Ganguli

CONTENTS

CHAPTER 1

INTRODUCTION

Pharmaceutical Analysis deals with the study of Analytical methods in testing of pharmaceutical products. Pharmaceutical Analysis covers all stages from raw materials to finished products. This is done with reference to various pharmacopoeias. In this book, all illustrations on titrimetric methods for analysis of drugs and pharmaceuticals to achieve high range of purity has been dealt. Because pure samples can only be used for manufacturing purpose. High range of quality is to be maintained throughout the process which starts from raw materials to finished product. So one must know the common types of titrimetric analysis to analyse a wide range of pharmaceutical products. Choice of titrimetric method depends on the nature of compounds and upon its physical and chemical properties. Based on these properties, titration method is selected which will provide accurate result in regard to purity of compound. Respective chapters of this book provide a detailed study on the principle involved in these titration studies. Procedure and calculations are provided for helping students to do practical work.

Chapter on Miscellaneous Analysis and Illustrative methods provide various procedure to perform analysis of pharmaceutical substances. This book is meant to fulfill the requirements of students to understand the basic concept of titrimetry. It is primarily written to stimulate interest of students in pharmaceutical analysis. Hence the core chapters deal with various methods for analysis purpose.

CHAPTER 2

ACID-BASE TITRATIONS

ACID-BASE CONCEPT

Definitions of Acid

- Acids react with bases to give salts and water.
- Acids react with metals liberating hydrogen.
- Acids react with calonates liberating CO_2.
- Acids turn blue litmus red.

Arrhenius discovered the electrolyte dissociation and stated that acids have general formula HX. This HX dissociates in solution to H^+ and X^- ions. Arrhenius considered bases have general formula MOH. This in solution dissociates to M^+ and OH^- ions.

The Arrhenius theory explains the behaviour of many acids and bases in aqueous solutions.

Bronsted and Lowry Concept

Acid is defined as a proton donor and base is proton acceptor.

Lewis Concept

This concept states that an electron-pair acceptor and a base is an electron-pair donor. Lewis acids are electrophilic agents and Lewis bases are nucleophilic agents.

Polyprotic or polybasic acids: Acids which can donate more than one proton or react with more than one mole of base are polyprotic or polybasic acids.

Polyacidic bases: Bases then can react with more than one mole of acids are known as Polyacidic bases.

Polyprotic acids may reach in stages, yielding salts with differing amounts of the base or hydrogen ions, e.g.,

$$H_3PO_4 + NaOH \longrightarrow H_2O + \underset{\text{(Primary or acid salt)}}{NaH_2PO_4}$$

$$NaH_2PO_4 + H_2O \longrightarrow \underset{\text{(Secondary salt)}}{Na_2HPO_4}$$

$$Na_2HPO_4 + NaOH \longrightarrow H_2O + \underset{\text{(Tertiary salt)}}{Na_3PO_4}$$

Phosphoric acid is a triprotic or tribasic acid.

STRENGTH OF ACIDS AND BASES

An acid is a substance which ionizes to yield hydrogen ions or protons. Base is a substance which combines with hydrogen ions.

So, an acid is a proton donor and a base is a proton acceptor.

$$\underset{\text{Acid}}{A} \rightleftharpoons H^+ + \underset{\text{Base}}{B}$$

Strength of an acid is related to the concentration of hydrogen ions which it yield upon ionization and will depend upon the value of the degree of dissociation, α, at any given concentration.

The acid dissociation constant, K_a provides a relationship between α and the concentration. It is a measure of the acid strength.

Similarly, the strength of a base is related to its dissociation constant.

$$\underset{\text{Acid}}{HA} \rightleftharpoons H^+ + \underset{\text{Conjugate Base}}{A^-}$$

$$A^- + H_2O \rightleftharpoons HA + OH^-$$

$$K_a = \frac{[H^+].[A^-]}{[HA]} \quad \text{and} \quad K_b = \frac{[HA].[OH^-]}{[A^-]}$$

$$K_a.K_b = \frac{[H^+].[A^-]}{[HA]} \cdot \frac{[HA].[OH^-]}{[A^-]}$$

$\therefore$ $K_a.K_b = [H^+]\,[OH^-]$

$\therefore$ $K_a.K_b = K_w$

Stronger the acid the weaker its conjugated base.

ELECTROLYTIC DISSOCIATION

Certain substances called electrolytes dissolve in water. This solution conducts electricity. In 1887, Arrhenius explained that this ability of electrolytes to conduct electricity is due to the fact that in solution, electrolytes undergo dissociation into positively and negatively charged fragments called ions. Positive ions move towards a negative electrode and negative ions move towards a positive electrode. The passage of ions and its neutralization, i.e., neutralization of ionic charges at the electrode causes conduction of electric current through the solution.

THE LAW OF MASS ACTION

This was first coined by Guldberg and Wage in 1867. The law is expressed as:

The rate of a chemical reaction is proportional to the active masses of the reacting substances. In dilute solutions, the active mass is the concentrate of the reacting species, i.e., gram-molecules or gram-ions per litre. The constant of proportionality is the velocity constant. Here, $A \longrightarrow B$ is a reaction;

$$\text{Rate of reaction} = K\,[A]$$

where $[A]$ = Concentrate of A

K = Velocity constant

Here, a homogeneous reversible reaction is considered

$$A + B \rightleftharpoons C + D$$

According to the law of mass action:

$$V_f = K_1\,[A].[B]$$

$$V_b = K_2\ [C].[D]$$

$$V_f = \text{Velocity of forward reaction}$$

$$V_b = \text{Velocity of backward reaction}$$

At equilibrium $V_f = V_b$

$$K_2\ [C].[D] = K_1\ [A].[B]$$

$$\frac{K_1}{K_2} = \frac{[C].[D]}{[A].[B]}$$

Since K_1 and K_2 are both constants, the fraction K_1/K_2 must also be a constant.

$$\therefore \qquad K = \frac{[C].[D]}{[A].[B]}$$

K = Equilibrium constant of the reaction

The equilibrium constant for the general reversible reaction is:

$$aA + bB + cC + \ldots\ldots\ldots \rightleftharpoons pP + qQ + rR + \ldots\ldots\ldots \text{ is}$$

$$K = \frac{[P]^P.[Q]^q.[R]^r}{[A]^a.[B]^b.[C]^c}$$

where a, b, c and p, q, r are the number of molecules of the reacting species.

Application of the law of mass action to solutions of weak electrolytes:

Strong electrolytes get completely dissociated even in less concentrated solutions, so they do not constitute equilibrium system.

Weak electrolyte are only incompletely dissociated even in favourable ionization conditions of dilute solution. So an equilibrium is considered in terms of the law of mass action which occurs between undissociated molecules and ions.

THE DISSOCIATION OF WATER

Water is a weak electrolyte. It is very slightly dissociated into its ions.

$$H_2O \rightleftharpoons H^+ + OH^-$$

From the law of mass action,

$$K = \frac{[H^+].[OH^-]}{[H_2O]}$$

In pure water and in aqueous solutions (dilute) the concentration of free water is constant.

$$\therefore \quad K_w = [H^+].[OH^-]$$

$$K_w = \text{Ionic product of water}$$

At ordinary experimental conditions,

$$K_w = 1 \times 10^{-14}$$

when the concentration of H^+ and OH^- ions are expressed in gram-ions/litre.

In pure water, $[H^+] = [OH^-]$

$$[H^+] = \sqrt{K_w}$$

$$= 10^{-7} \text{ gram-ions/litre}$$

Solutions in which H^+ concentration is greater than 10^{-7} are acidic in nature. If H^+ concentration is less than 10^{-7} then the solution is alkaline.

THE HYDROGEN ION EXPONENT (pH)

pH is the negative logarithm (to base 10) of the concentration of hydrogen ions in solution:

$$pH = -\log_{10}[H^+] = \log_{10}\frac{1}{[H^+]}$$

A neutral solution is one where pH = 7

An acid solution is one where pH = < 7

An alkaline solution is one where pH = > 7.

COMMON ION EFFECT

The concentration of a particular ion in an ionic reaction is increased by the addition of a compound which gives that ion on dissociation. This means that the particular ion is thus obtained from the compound present in solution and is also obtained from the added reagent, that's why the name 'common ion' is given.

For example: $NH_4OH \xrightarrow{H_2O} NH_4^+ + OH^-$

$$H_2O \longrightarrow H^+ + OH^-$$

Here excess of OH^- ions is present. This system has excess of hydroxyl ion. Some of the hydroxyl ion combines with NH_4^+ ion to form ammonium hydroxide. OH^- ion is the common ion. This is the common ion effect.

IONIC PRODUCT OF WATER

Kohlrausch and Heydweiller found in 1894 that the most highly purified water possesses a small and definite conductivity. So water must be highly ionized as per the equation:

$$H_2O \rightleftharpoons H^+ + OH^-$$

As per the Law of Mass Action, the following equation is obtained at any given temperature.

$$\frac{{}^aH^+ \times {}^aOH^-}{{}^aH_2O} = \frac{[H^-].[OH^-]}{[H_2O]} \times \frac{{}^yH^+ . {}^yOH^-}{{}^yH_2O}$$

Water is only slightly ionized, so the ionic concentration is small and their activity coefficient is unity. The activity of the unionised molecules is also taken as unity.

So the expression is:

$$\frac{[H^+][OH^-]}{[H_2O]} = \text{a constant}$$

In pure water or in dilute solutions, the concentration of the undissociated water is considered constant.

$$\therefore \quad [H^+] \times [OH^-] = K_w$$

K_w = Ionic product of water.

The ionic product varies with the temperature. At 25°C, its value is taken as 1×10^{-14}. This value is constant in dilute solutions. If the product of $[H^+]$ and $[OH^-]$ in aqueous solution exceeds this value, the excess ions will immediately combine to form water. On the contrary, if the product of two ionic concentrations is less than 10^{-14}, more water molecules will dissociate until the equilibrium value is obtained.

Henderson-Hasselbalch Equation

The change in pH upon the addition of an acid or base and the pH of a buffer solution is calculated by buffer equation. This buffer equation is calculated by considering the effect of a salt on the ionization of a weak acid if the salt and the acid have an ion in common.

BUFFERS AND BUFFER SOLUTIONS

If a small quantity of hydrochloric acid is added to purified water, a significant increase in H^+ concentration occurs quickly. In the same way if a small quantity of sodium hydroxide is added to pure water, it results in large increase in OH^- concentrate. These variations take place because water alone cannot neutralize the traces of acid or base, i.e., it has no ability to resists the changes in H^+ concentrate or pH of the solution or solvent. So, water is unbuffered.

Such substances or combinations of substances are known as buffers which has the ability to resist changes in pH. This type of action is known as buffer action. This buffer action efficiency is measured by a function known as buffer capacity. These solutions are called buffer solutions. So, buffer solutions are the systems usually an aqueous solution that has the capacity to resist changes in pH upon addition of small amounts of a strong acid or base.

Buffer solutions are usually made up of a weak acid and a salt of the acid or a weak base and a salt of the base. For example, acetic acid and sodium acetate and the other one is ammonium hydroxide and ammonium chloride mixture. Other examples are boric acid and sodium borate and disodium phosphate and sodium acid phosphate.

Buffer solutions are used in the preparation of:

(i) Dosage forms such as injections and opthalmic solutions which are given directly to pH sensitive body fluids.

(ii) In pharmaceutical analysis where pH adjustments are required.

While selecting a buffer system, emphasis must be given to the dissociation constant of the weak acid or base to produce maximum buffer capacity. The dissociation constant of an acid is a measure of the strength of the acid. That is, the more readily the acid dissociates, the higher is the dissociation constant and stronger is the acid. The same is with bases also.

Consider the following equation:

$$\because \quad HA \rightleftharpoons H^+ + A^-$$

$$K_a = \frac{[H^+][A^-]}{[HA]}$$

Here, A^- = Salt and HA = acid.

This equation is the dissociation constant or K_a value of a weak acid.

Since the numeric values of most of the dissociation constants are small numbers and can vary over many powers of 10, so they are expressed as negative logarithms, i.e.,

$$pK_a = -\log K_a$$

$$\text{Equation } K_a = \frac{[H^+].[A^-]}{[HA]}$$

If expressed is logarithmic form then:

$$pK_a = -\log [H^+] - \log \frac{\text{salt}}{\text{acid}}$$

$$\because \quad pH = -\log [H^+]$$

$$\therefore \quad pK_a = pH - \log \frac{\text{salt}}{\text{acid}}$$

$$\therefore \quad pH = pK_a + \log \frac{\text{salt}}{\text{acid}}$$

This equation is **Henderson-Hasselbalch equation** for weak acids. This is also known as buffer equation.

Similarly the dissociation constant or K_b value of a weak base is

$$K_b = \frac{[B^+].[OH^-]}{[BOH]}$$

Here B^+ = salt and BOH = base.

Buffer equation for weak bases is:

$$pH = pK_w - pK_b + \log \frac{\text{base}}{\text{salt}}$$

The buffer equation has following uses:

(i) Calculation of pH of a buffer system if composition is known.

(ii) To calculate the molar ratio of the components of a buffer system to give a solution of desired pH.

(iii) To calculate the change in pH of a buffered solution upon addition of trace amount of acid or base.

Ionization of acetic acid is considered:

$$HAc + H_2O \rightleftharpoons H_3O^+ + Ac^-$$

$$K_a = \frac{[H_3O^+][Ac^-]}{[HAc]} = 1.75 \times 10^{-5}$$

$$[H_3O^+] = K_a \frac{[HA_c]}{[Ac^-]}$$

$$[H_3O^+] = K_a \left[\frac{\text{acid}}{\text{salt}}\right]$$

$$-\log [H_3O^+] = -\log K_a - \log [\text{acid}] + \log [\text{salt}]$$

$$pH = pK_a + \log \frac{[\text{salt}]}{[\text{acid}]}$$

(This is the buffer equation or **Henderson-Hasselbalch equation.**)

The buffer equation for solutions of weak bases and their salts is derived from:

$$[OH^-] = K_b \frac{[base]}{[salt]}$$

$$[OH^-] = \frac{K_w}{[H_3O^+]}$$

$$pH = pK_w - pK_b + \log \frac{[base]}{[salt]}$$

Example: $H^+ + A^- \longrightarrow HA$

$$OH^- + HA \rightleftharpoons H_2O + A^-$$

NEUTRALIZATION CURVES

Neutralization process are studied by studying the changes in the hydrogen ion concentrate during the course of titration. The curve obtained by plotting pH as the ordinate against the percentage of acid neutralized (or the number of ml of alkali added) as abscissa is the **Neutralization or Titration Curve.**

Examples:

Neutralization of a Strong Acid with a Strong Base

Here the titration of 100 ml of 1 M HCl with 1 M sodium hydroxide solution is considered, the pH of 1 M HCl is 0. When 50 ml of 1 M base is added then 50 ml of unneutralised 1 M acid is present in a total volume of 150 ml.

On addition of 100 ml of base, the pH changes sharply to 7, i.e., the theoretical equivalence point is reached. This is sodium chloride solution. Any amount of sodium hydroxide added will be in excess of that needed for neutralization (Fig. 2.1).

Neutralization of a Weak Acid with a Strong Base

Here neutralization of 100 ml of 0.1 M acetic acid with 0.1 M sodium hydroxide solution is considered. The pH of the solution at equivalence point is 8.72. After the equivalence point have been passed the solution contain excess of OH^- ions. Here pH is due to the excess of base present so the titration curve coincides with that for 0.1 M HCl (Fig. 2.2).

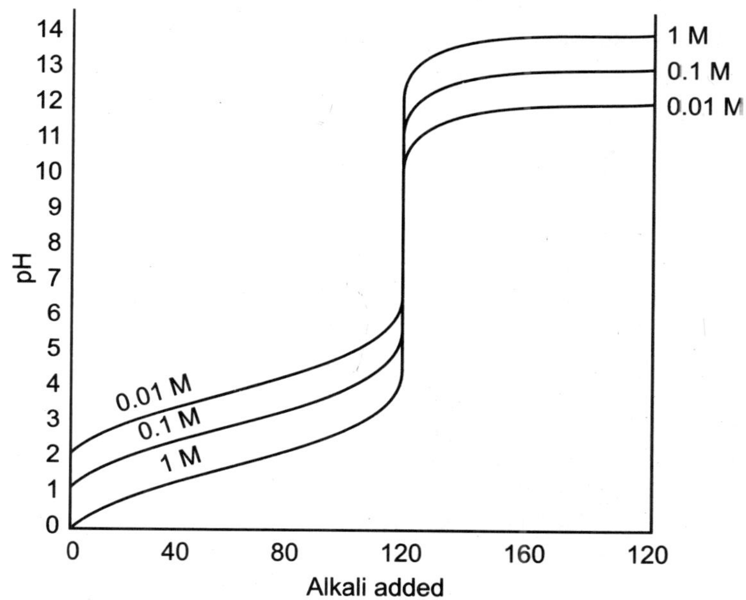

Fig. 2.1: *Neutralisation curves of 100 ml of HCl with NaOH of same concentration*

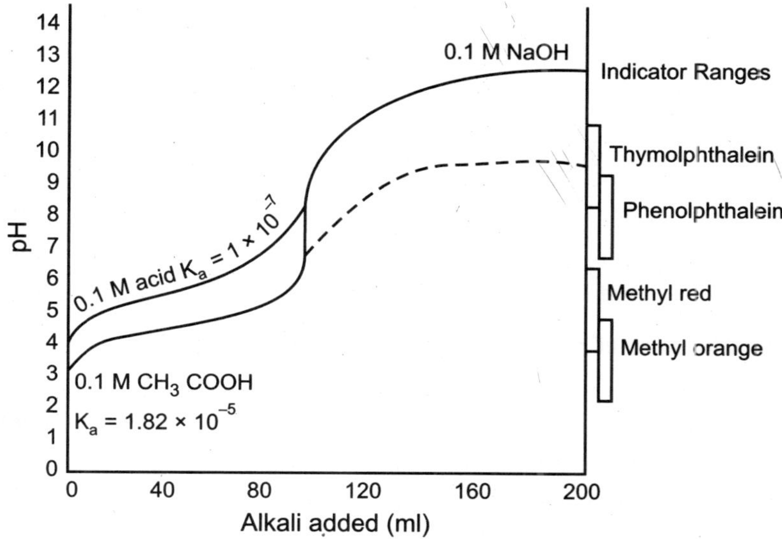

Fig. 2.2: *Neutralisation curve of 100 ml of 0.1 M AcOH ($K_a = 1.82 \times 10^{-5}$) and ($K_a = 1 \times 10^{-7}$) with 0.1 M NaOH*

Neutralization of a Weak Base with a Strong Acid

Here the titration of 100 ml of 0.1 M aqueous NH_3 ($K_b = 1.85 \times 10^{-5}$) with 0.1 M HCl is considered. The pH of the solution at the equivalence point is 5.28. After the equivalence point is reached the solution contains excess of H^+ ions, so the hydrolysis of salt gets suppressed. The resultant pH changes is due to excess of acid present.

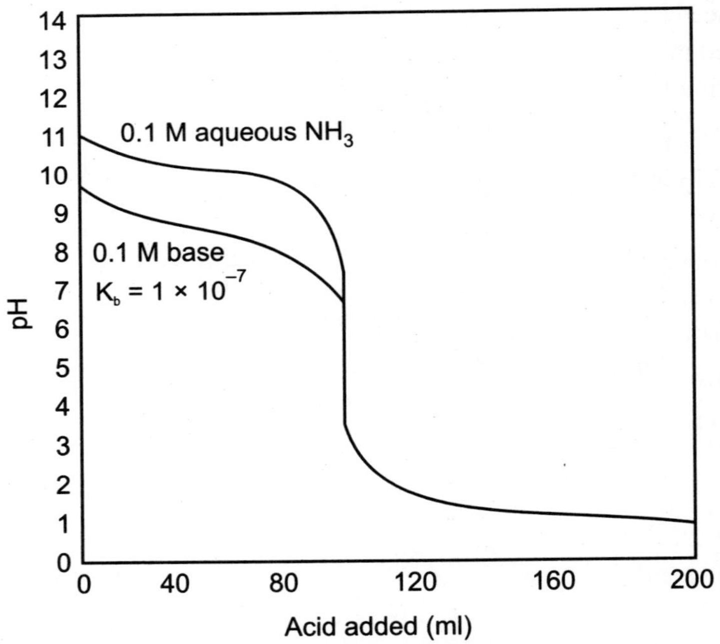

Fig. 2.3: *Neutralisation curve of 100 ml 0.1 M aqueous NH_3 ($K_a = 1.8 \times 10^{-5}$) and of 0.1 M base ($K_a = 1 \times 10^{-7}$) with 0.1 M HCl*

Neutralization of a Weak Acid With a Weak Base

Here the titration of 100 ml of 0.1 M acetic acid ($K_a = 1.82 \times 10^{-5}$) with 0.1 M aqueous ammonia ($K_b = 1.8 \times 10^{-5}$) is considered. The pH at the equivalence point is 7.1.

The neutralization curve upto the equivalence point is identical with that of 0.1 M NaOH solution as base. After this point, the titration resembles the addition of 0.1 M aqueous NH_3 solution to 0.1 M ammonium acetate solution. Here in neutralization of a weak acid with a weak base, the change in pH near the equivalence point and the whole of the neutralization curve is very gradual. There is no sudden change in pH in this reaction. So, no sharp end point can be obtained with any simple indicator. So, mixed indicator is used. Mixed indicator exhibits a sharp colour change over a limited pH range is suitable. Hence for acetic acid-ammonia solution titrations neutral red-methylene blue mixed indicator is used. But it is better to avoid the use of indicators in titration of weak acid and a weak base.

Neutralization of a Polyprotic and with a Strong Base

The shape of titration curves depend on the magnitude of the dissociation constants.

For a diprotic acid, if the difference between primary and secondary dissociation constants is large, i.e., $K_1/K_2 > 10000$, the solution becomes a mixture of two acids with K_1 and K_2 as their constants.

Examples:

(1) For sulphurous acid, $K_1 = 1.7 \times 10^{-2}$ and $K_2 = 1.0 \times 10^{-7}$. There is a sharp change of pH near the first equivalence point but for second equivalence point, the change is less marked.

(2) For carbonic acid, $K_1 = 4.3 \times 10^{-7}$ and $K_2 = 5.6 \times 10^{-11}$. Here also the first stage is sharp in the neutralization curve, but the second stage is far too weak to exhibit any point of inflexion. There is no suitable indicator for direct titration.

(3) Here, triprotic acid is considered. This is phosphoric (V) acid (orthophosphoric acid). Here, $K_1 = 7.5 \times 10^{-3}$, $K_2 = 6.2 \times 10^{-8}$ and $K_3 = 5 \times 10^{-13}$.

Here,
$$K_1/K_2 = 1.2 \times 10^{+5}$$
$$K_2/K_3 = 1.2 \times 10^{5}$$

Here the acid behaves as a mixture of three monoprotic acids with the dissociation constants given above. Neutralization occurs almost completely to the end of the primary stage. Then secondary stage starts and it proceeds to completion before the tertiary stage commences and is apparent.

- pH at first equivalence point is 4.6.
- pH at second equivalence point is 9.7.
- Third stage is very weak, the curve is very flat and no indicator is available for direct titration.

The third equivalence point is calculated from the equation written below:

$$pH = \frac{1}{2}\ pK_w + \frac{1}{2}\ pK_a - \frac{1}{2}\ pc$$

$$= 7.0 + 6.15 - \frac{1}{2}\ (1.6)$$

$$= 12.35 \text{ for } 0.1\ M\ H_3Po_4$$

The figure is shown below:

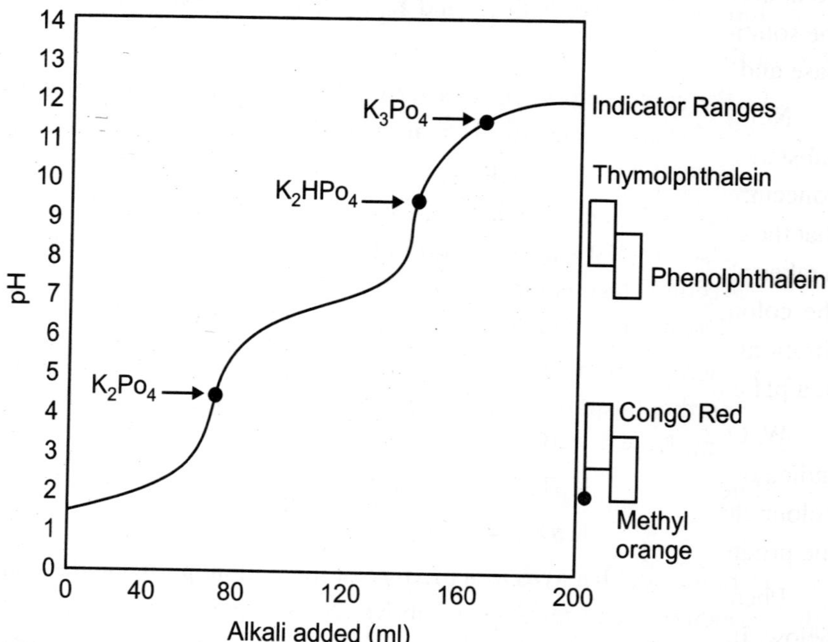

Fig. 2.4: *Titration of 50 ml of 0.1 M H_3Po_4 with 0.1 M KOH.*

ACID BASE INDICATORS AND THEIR CHOICE

Titration of an alkaline solution with a standard solution of an acid is the determination of the amount of acid that is chemically equivalent to the amount of base present. This point is known as equivalence point, stoichiometric point or theoretical end point. The resultant aqueous solution contains salt.

If both acid and base are strong electrolytes then the solution at the end-point is neutral. The pH at this point is 7.

In other case, when either the acid or base is a weak electrolyte then the salt gets hydrolysed to a certain degree. The solution at the equivalence point will be either slightly alkaline or slightly acidic in nature. The exact pH at the end-point or equivalence point of the solution is to be calculated from the ionization constant of the weak acid or the weak base and also from the concentration of the solution. The correct end point is characterized by the value of the hydrogen ion concentration of the solution. This pH value depends upon the nature of the acid and the base and also upon the concentration of the solution.

Neutralization indicators or acid-base indicators are a type of substances that change colour according to the pH or hydrogen ion concentration of the solution. The main property of these indicators is that the change of colour from acid side to alkaline side is not quick but it takes place within a small interval of pH, i.e., about 2 pH units. This is the colour change interval of the indicator. In case of the acid-base titrations an indicator is selected which exhibits a distinct colour change at a pH close to its equivalence point.

W. Ostwald proposed the concept of indicators. He suggested that indicators in general use are very weak organic acids or bases. The colour change of indicators is due to structural changes which includes the production of quinonoid and resonance forms.

Phenolphthalein indicator is considered. The figure I to IV are given below. In the presence of dilute alkali the lactone ring in I opens and forms II structure. Triphenylcarbinol structure II undergoes loss of water to produce the resonating ion III. This resonating ion III is red in colour. If phenolphthalein is treated with excess of concentrated alcoholic alkali, the red colour which was produced firstly disappears due to the formation of IV.

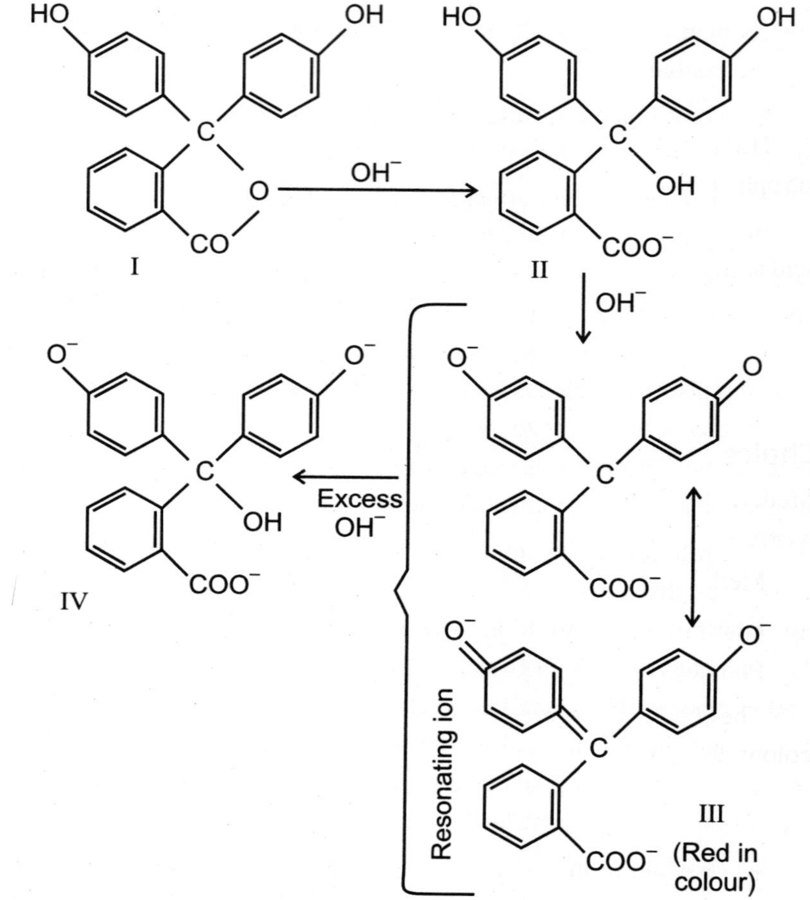

HO OH HO OH

C C

O OH^- OH

CO I COO^- II

OH^-

O^- O^- O^- O

C C

Excess OH^- OH

COO^- IV COO^-

O^- O^-

Resonating ion C

III

COO^- (Red in colour)

THEORY OF INDICATORS

The theory suggests that the colour is organic compounds is due to the presence of some unsaturated 'chromophores' like C = O, C = C, N = O and N = N. These chromophores are intensified by 'auxochromes' like NH_2 and OH groups. The colour change of many indicators is due to the transformation of a benzenoid structure into a quinonoid and *vice versa*, along with the change in H^+ concentrate of the solution.

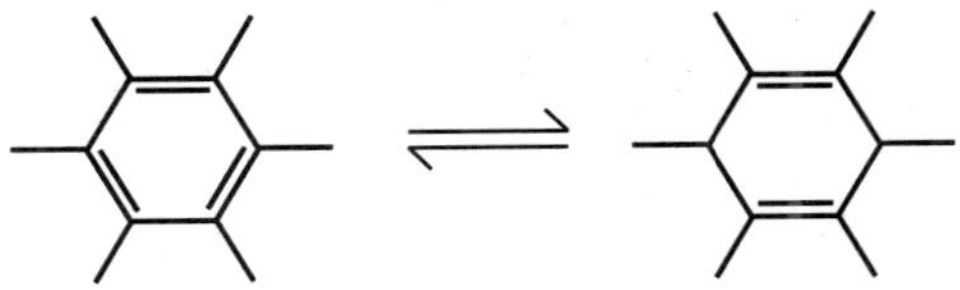

Benzenoid form (Colourless) ⇌ Quinonoid form (Coloured)

H.E. Armstrong explained this case by taking the example of nitrophenols.

In alkaline solution *p*-nitrophenol is present as the yellow ion. But in acid solution, it is found as colourless nitrocompound.

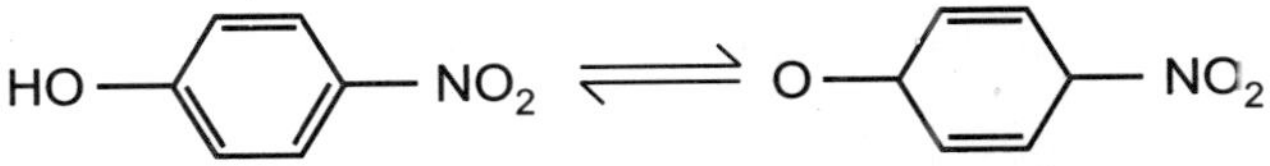

HO—C₆H₄—NO_2 ⇌ O—C₆H₄—NO_2

Almost colourless / Deep yellow

Choice of Acid-Base Indicators

Methyl orange is used in the assay of strong acids and in reactions where CO_2 is evolved. CO_2 does not affect this indicator.

Methyl red is used in the assay of weak bases.

Example: Ammonia and amines.

Phenolphthalein is used in the assay of weak acids.

The choice of some well known indicators along with their pH ranges, colour changes are summarized below:

1. **Congo red:** It is sodium salt of an azo compound. Its pH range is 3-5 causes blue colour to become red.
2. **Dimethyl yellow:** It is 4-dimethylamino-azobenzene. Its pH range is 2.8 – 4.0. It turns red to yellow. It gives letter end-point in strongly alcoholic solution. It is used in the determination of carvone.
3. **Methyl orange:** It is the sodium salt of 4-dimethylamino azobenzene-4′-sulphonic acid. Its pH range is 2.8–4.0. It turns red colour to yellow. A 0.04% aqueous alcoholic solution is used.

4. **Methyl red:** It is 4′-dimethylamino azobenzene-2-carboxylic acid.

Its pH range is 4.2-6.3. It turns red colour to yellow colour. The preparation of this indicator is described in pharmacopoeia. This methyl red indicator is used in place of methyl orange in the titration of NH_3 and other weak bases where it gives a better end-point.

Phenolphthalein

It turns colourless to red. It acts in the pH between 8.3-10.0. The colour limit of red varies with the concentration of the indicator. Generally, a 1% solution in alcohol is used in titrations.

SULPHONPHTHALEIN INDICATORS

Clark and Lubs introduced this sulphonphthalein indicator. It is similar to phenolphthalein. Here $-SO_3H$ group takes the place of $-CO_2H$ group. Example of sulphonphthalein indicator is phenolsulphonphthalein (phenol red).

Some examples of sulphonphthalein indicators are:

1. **Bromocresol green:** It is tetrabromo-m-cresol-sulphonphthalein. Its pH range is 3.6-5.2. It changes yellow colour to blue.
2. **Bromocresol purple:** It is dibromo-o-cresol-sulphonphthalein. Its pH range is 5.2-6.8. It changes yellow colour to purple.
3. **Thymol blue:** It is thymolsulphonphthalein. Acid range covers 1.2-2.8. Colour changes from red to yellow.

Alkaline range covers 8.0-9.6. It turns yellow colour to blue.

Bromophenol blue: It is tetrabromophenolsulphonphthalein. Its pH range is 2.8-4.6, colour changes from yellow to blue.

Bromothymol blue: It is dibromothymol-sulphonphthalein. Its pH range is 6.0-7.6. Colour changes from yellow to blue.

Phenol red: It is phenolsulphonphthalein. Its pH range is 6.8-8.4. Its colour changes from yellow to red.

It helps in titrating certain weak acids in presence of alcohol which does not affect its colour change.

Cresol red: It is o-cresolsulphonphthalein. Acid range is 0.2-1.8. Red-yellow alkaline range is 7.2-8.8 changes yellow to red.

Methyl orange is a type of azo indicator. In alkaline solution, it is yellow and is present as the sodium salt of a sulphonic acid. Yellow colour is due to —N:N— group. When acid is added, structural changes occur to a red quinonoid form.

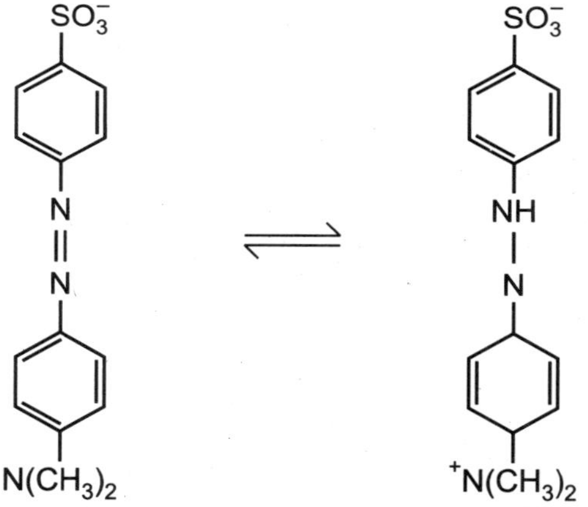

SO_3^- … $N=N$ … $N(CH_3)_2$ ⇌ SO_3^- … $NH-N$ … $^+N(CH_3)_2$

Azoid form, yellow in neutral or alkaline solution

Quinonoid form red in acid solution

SCREENED INDICATOR

A screened indicator solution contains dye which does not change in colour in the pH range involved. This is used to modify the acidic and alkaline colours of the indicator by light absorption. This gives a sharp end-point. Screened methyl red which is methyl red with methylene blue is preferred in certain pharmacopoeial assays. Its range the same range as unscreened methyl red. Its colour change is from red-violet in acid solution to green in alkaline solution.

Screened methyl orange is methyl orange with xylene cyanol FF is another type of screened indicator. Here the colour changes from magenta through grey at pH of 3.8. Then it changes to green in alkaline solution.

MIXED INDICATORS

In some cases it is required to have a sharp colour change in a narrow and selected range of pH. This does not occur with an ordinary acid base indicator as the colour change extends over two units of pH. This condition is achieved by a mixture of indicators. Mixed indicators are selected so that their pK_{in} values are close together and the overlapping colours are complementary at an intermediate pH value. The examples are given below:

(i) A mixture of equal parts of neutral red (0.1% solution in ethanol) and methylene blue (0.1% solution in ethanol) provides a sharp colour change from violet-blue to green. This occur from acid to alkaline solution at pH 7.

This indicator is used to titrate acetic acid with NH_3 solution and *vice versa.*

(ii) A mixture of thymol blue (3 parts of a 0.1% aqueous solution of the sodium salt) and cresol red (1 part of a 0.1% aqueous solution of the sodium salt) changes its colour from yellow to violet at pH 8.3. This indicator is used for the titration of carbonate to hydrogen carbonate stage.

Buffer action in a solution of a weak acid and its salt is due to the fact that H^+ ions are removed by the anions of a weak acid to form unionized molecules.

Example:

$$H^+ + A^- \rightleftharpoons HA$$

$$OH^- + HA \rightleftharpoons H_2O + A^-$$

The above equation shows that hydroxyl ions are also eliminated by neutralisation.

The concentration of hydrogen ions as compared to those of the weak acid and its salt in that type of buffer solution is determined by the dissociation constant of the acid. The expression is given below:

$$K_a = \frac{[H^+][A^-]}{[HA]}$$

$$\therefore \quad \log K_a = \log [H^+] + \log \frac{[A^-]}{[HA]}$$

$$\therefore \quad -\log K_a = -\log [H^+] - \log \frac{[A^-]}{[HA]}$$

$$\therefore \quad pK_a = pH - \log \frac{[A^-]}{[HA]}$$

$$\therefore \quad pH = pK_a + \log \frac{[A^-]}{[HA]}$$

The acid HA is a weak acid. So it only gets slightly ionized. Ionization of the acid is repressed by the large concentration of anions A^- from the fully dissociated salt.

Therefore, [HA] is numerically equal to the initial concentration of acid and $[A^-]$ is numerically equal to the initial concentration of salt.

$$\therefore \quad pH = pK_a + \log \frac{[salt]}{[acid]}$$

(Henderson equation)

If salt = acid then the above equation becomes:

$$pH = pK_a + \log 1$$

$$\therefore \quad pH = pK_a$$

A ten fold increase or decrease in the ratio of [salt/acid] raises or lowers the pH of the solution by one pH unit. Buffer capacity is the resistance of a buffer solution to such a pH change. Buffer capacity is defined as the number of gram equivalents of strong acid or strong alkali that is necessary to produce a change of 1 pH unit in 1 litre of the solution.

A Study of the Buffer Mixture of a Weak Base and its Salt

This type of buffer solution is considered, hydroxyl ions are removed by the salt cations (BH^+) to form unionized molecules:

$$OH^- + BH^+ \longrightarrow B + H_2O$$

Hydrogen ions are also removed by neutralization process, the reaction is given below:

$$H^+ + B \longrightarrow BH^+$$

The concentration of weak base and its salt relative to that of hydroxyl ion in the solution can be determined by the dissociation constant of the base, i.e.,

$$K_b = \frac{[BH^+][OH^-]}{[B]}$$

$$\therefore \quad \log K_b = \log [OH^-] + \log \frac{[BH^+]}{[B]}$$

$$\therefore \quad -\log K_b = \log [OH^-] - \log \frac{[BH^+]}{[B]}$$

$$\therefore \quad pK_b = pOH - \log \frac{[BH^+]}{[B]}$$

But, $pOH = pK_w - pH$

$$\therefore \quad pK_b = pK_w - pH - \log \frac{[BH^+]}{[B]}$$

$$pH = pK_w - pK_b - \log \frac{[BH^+]}{[B]}$$

The base B is weak and is only slightly ionised.

The ionization of base B is repressed by the relatively large concentration of cations BH^+ which is obtained from the fully dissociated salt.

$\therefore$ $[BH^+]$ is numerically = to initial concentrate of salt

[B] is numerically = to initial concentrate of base

$$\therefore \quad pH = pK_w - pK_b - \log \frac{[salt]}{[base]}$$

$$pK_w - pK_b = pK_a$$

$$\because \quad pH = pK_a - \log \frac{[acid]}{[salt]}$$

$$pH = pK \frac{[salt]}{[base]}$$

BH^+ is conjugated acid of base B.

NEUTRALIZATION INDICATORS

The equivalence point in the titration of standard acids and alkalis are not always the point of exact neutrality (pH 7.0). Equivalent point and exact neutrality is attained only in strong acid and strong base titrations. If weak acid or weak base is used then the resulting salt will be hydrolysed. The resultant solution will be either acidic or alkaline respectively. In this case, the actual pH of the solution at the end point is determined potentiometrically and also by a neutralization indicator. The indicator changes colour according to the H^+ concentrate of the solution.

Indicators are weak acids or weak bases in nature. They have different colours in their conjugate base and acid forms (two colour indicators). Other indicators are one colour indicators and have one form coloured and the conjugate form is colourless. The following example is for an indicator functioning as a weak acid.

$$\underset{\text{Unionised colour}}{HI_n} \rightleftharpoons H^+ + \underset{\text{Inoised colour}}{I_n^-}$$

In acid solution, the excess of H^+ ions will depress the ionization of the indicator. Here the concentrate the I_n^- will be small and that of HI_n will be large. So the colour will be that of the unionized form. Alkali will cause removal of H^+ ions from the system with a increase in the concentrate of the ionized form I_n^-. As a result, the solution acquires the ionized colour.

$$\therefore \quad K_{Ina} = \frac{[H^+][I_n^-]}{[HI_n]}$$

$$[H^+] = K_{Ina} \frac{[HI_n]}{[I_n]}$$

$$\therefore \quad -\log [H^+] = -\log K_{Ina} - \log \frac{[HI_n]}{[I_n^-]}$$

$$\therefore \qquad pH = pK_{Ina} + \log \frac{[In^-]}{[HI_n]}$$

In the similar manner, an indicator functioning as a weak base, the following equilibrium will apply.

$$\underset{\text{Unionised colour}}{I_n} + H_2O \rightleftharpoons \underset{\text{Ionised colour}}{I_nH^+} + OH^-$$

$$K_{Inb} = \frac{[I_nH^+][OH^-]}{[I_n]}$$

$$\therefore \qquad pH = pK_w - pK_{Inb} - \log \frac{[I_nH^+]}{[I_n]}$$

TAUTOMERIC NEUTRALIZATION INDICATORS

The colour changes are being brought about by tautomeric changes in the structure of the molecule.

Example: Phenolphthalein indicator is solution is considered:

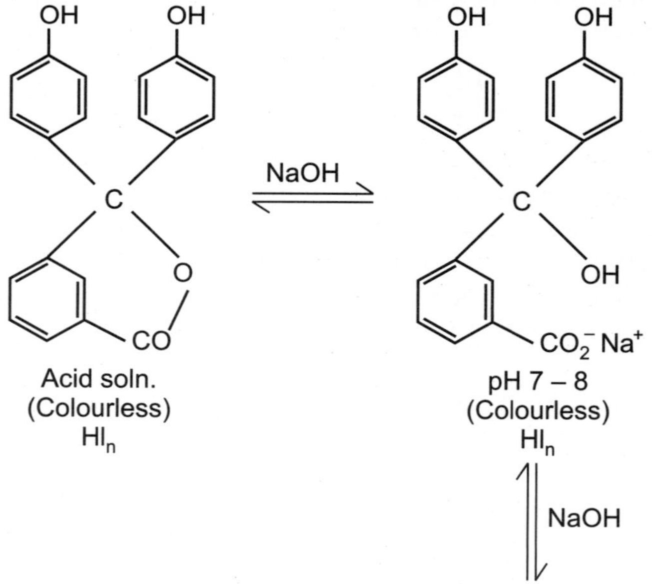

OH OH C O CO

NaOH ⇌

OH OH C OH CO_2^- Na^+

Acid soln.
(Colourless)
HI_n

pH 7 – 8
(Colourless)
HI_n

⇅ NaOH

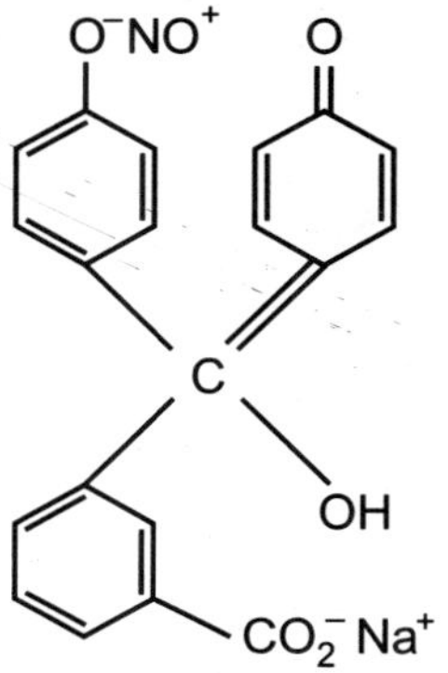

O^-NO^+ O

C

OH

$CO_2^- Na^+$

pH 8 – 10 (Red)

Red colour in alkaline solution is because of the formation of Quinonoid Structure.

This increases the possibility of resonance between the various ionic forms.

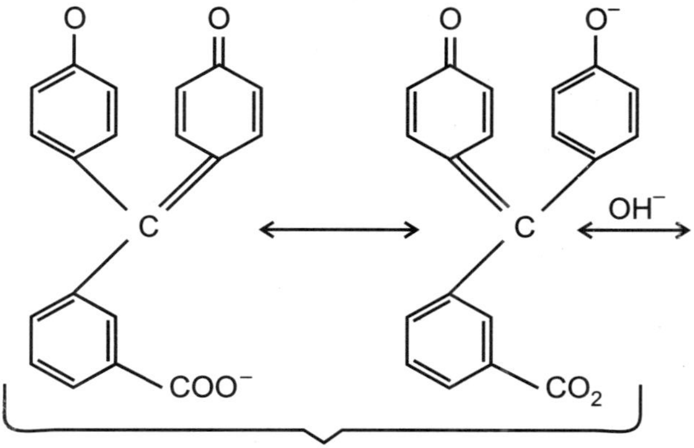

O O O O^-

C ⟷ C $\overset{OH^-}{\longleftrightarrow}$

COO^- CO_2

Coloured (I_n^-)

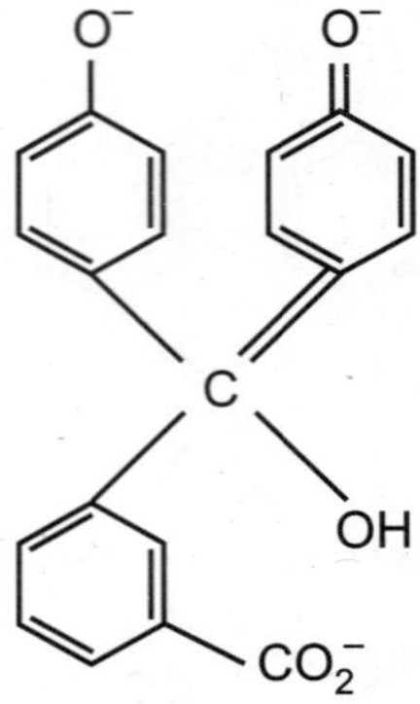

Colourless
pH12

$$\therefore \qquad pH = pK_{Ina} + \log \frac{[I_n^-]}{[HI_n]}$$

The average colour change interval, range an indicator is about two pH units.

CHAPTER 3

OXIDATION-REDUCTION TITRATIONS

Oxidation is the addition of oxygen and removal of hydrogen.

Example: $SO_2 + O \longrightarrow SO_3$

$H_2S + O \longrightarrow S + H_2O$

Reduction is the addition of hydrogen or removal of oxygen.

$C_2H_2 + 2H \longrightarrow C_2H_4$

$CuO + 2H \longrightarrow Cu + H_2O$

Oxidation-reduction titration are explained with reference to the loss or gain of electrons. That is, oxidation is loss of electrons and reduction is gain of electrons. In Redox systems, this process takes place simultaneously methods based on the gain or loss of electrons between oxidant and reductant are linked to the concept of equivalents. So, the expression of concentration is in terms of normality.

$$\text{Oxidised form} + ne \longrightarrow \text{Reduced form}$$

PHARMACEUTICAL APPLICATIONS

(i) It involves titrations to find the % purity of various pharmaceutical agents.

(ii) Pharmaceuticals like ascorbic acid tablets, tablets of ferrous fumarate, ferrous gluconate and ferrous succinate.

(iii) Iron-dextron injection, Iron-sorbitol injections and Tocopheryl acetate are assayed by Redox Titration method.

Strength and Equivalent Weight of Oxidizing and Reducing Agents

The concentrations of standard volumetric solutions are expressed in terms of normality. Normality is obtained from the equivalent weights of the reacting substances. Now-a-days, must of the National and International drug standards compendia have changed the method of expressing concentrations from Normality to Molarity.

Normality: A normal solution (symbolized as N) contains 1 gm equivalent of substance per litre of solutions.

Example: 2 N is twice normal, 0.1 N or N/10 is Deci-normal and 0.01 N or N/100 is Centi-normal.

EQUIVALENT WEIGHT

The equivalent weight of a substance is calculated by the actual reaction which takes place. The equivalent weight of an Acid or Base is that weight of the substance which contains 1.0079 g of replaceable H (or its equivalent such as the OH group). So, the equivalent weights of HCl and NaOH are equal to their molecular weights.

On the other hand, the equivalent weight of H_2SO_4 or oxalic acid $[(COOH)_2]$ are half of their molecular weights as they contain two replaceable hydrogens.

In Oxidation-Reduction titrations, the equivalent weight is that weight which yields or combines with 1.0079 g of available hydrogen or 7.9997 g of available oxygen. The term available means available for use in the Redox Reaction under consideration.

Strength and Equivalent Weights of Oxidizing and Reducing Agents

The equivalence of an oxidizing or reducing agent is defined as the mass of the reagent which reacts with or contains 1.008 g of available

H or 8.000 g of available oxygen. The term available denotes the capable of being utilized or consumed in the process of oxidation or reduction reactions.

The amount of available oxygen is shown by the equation:

$$MnO^-_4 + 8H^+ + 5e \longrightarrow Mn^2 + 4H_2O$$

The equivalent is $KMnO_4/5$.

In case of $K_2Cr_2O_7$ (i.e., potassium dichromate) in acid solution, the equation becomes:

$$Cr_2O_7^2 + 14H^+ + 6e \longrightarrow 2Cr^3 + 7H_2O$$

The equivalent is $K_2Cr_2O_7/6$. The oxidation of Iron (II) chloride by chlorine in aqueous solution is written as:

$$2FeCl_2 + Cl_2 \longrightarrow 2FeCl_3$$

Ionically, it is expressed as:

$$2Fe^2 + Cl_2 = 2Fe^{3+} + 2Cl^-$$

The ion Fe^{2+} on conversion into another ion, i.e., Fe^{3+} is an example of oxidation. The neutral chlorine molecule is converted into negatively charged chloride ions Cl^- (reduction). Here the conversion of Fe^{2+} into Fe^{3+} requires loss of one electron. Neutral chlorine molecule gets converted to negatively charged chloride ions Cl^-.

Oxidation process involves a loss of electrons

$$Fe^{2+} - e \longrightarrow Fe^{3+}$$

Reduction involves gain of electrons

$$Cl_2 + 2e \longrightarrow 2Cl^-$$

In Oxidation-Reduction process or redox process electrons are transferred from the reducing agent to oxidizing agent.

So, an oxidizing agent is a substance that gains electrons and is reduced. A reducing agent is one that loses electrons and is oxidized.

The change in the number of electrons per ion in any oxidation-reduction process helps in calculating equivalent.

So, the equivalent of an oxidant or a reductant is the mole divided by the number of electrons which 1 mole of the substance gains or loses in reaction process.

Some examples are cited below:

(1) $MnO_4^- + 8H^+ + 5e \rightleftharpoons Mn^{2+} + 4H_2O$

(2) $Cr_2O_7^{2-} + 14H^+ + 6e \rightleftharpoons 2Cr^{3+} + 7H_2O$

(3) $Fe^{2+} \rightleftharpoons Fe^{3+} + e$

Ionic equations for use in calculation of the equivalents of oxidizing and reducing agents:

Oxidants (Oxidizing Agent)	Partial Ionic Equation
1. $KMnO_4$ (acid)	$MnO_4^- + 8H^+ + 5e \rightleftharpoons Mn^{2+} + 4H_2O$
2. $KMnO_4$ (neutral)	$MnO_4^- + 2H_2O + 3e \rightleftharpoons MnO_2 + 4OH^-$
3. $KMnO_4$ (strongly alkaline)	$MnO_4^- + e \rightleftharpoons MnO_4^{2-}$
4. Bromine	$Br_2 + 2e \rightleftharpoons 2Br^-$
5. Iodine	$I_2 + 2e \rightleftharpoons 2I^-$

Reductants (Reducing Agent)	Partial Ionic Equation
1. Sodium thiosulphate	$2S_2O_3^{2-} \rightleftharpoons S_4O_6^{2-} + 2e$
2. Oxalic acid	$C_2O_4^{2-} \rightleftharpoons 2CO_2 + 2e$
3. Zinc	$Zn \rightleftharpoons Zn^{2+} + 2e$
4. Hydrogen peroxide	$H_2O_2 \rightleftharpoons 2H^+ + O_2 + 2e$

$$Eq. = MnO_4^-/5 = KMnO_4/5$$

$$Eq. = Cr_2O_7^{2-}/6 = K_2Cr_2O_7/6$$

$$Eq. = Fe^{2+}/1 = FeSO_4/1$$

MEASUREMENT OF ELECTRODE POTENTIAL

Oxidimetry involves oxidation-reduction reactions associated with transfer of electrons. In this process, the valence of an oxidized atom or ion is increased while the valence of a reduced atom or ion is decreased.

The direction of an oxidation-reduction reaction is predicted in case of some quantitative characteristic of the relative force of the oxidizing and reducing agents involved is known. This property is called as Redox potential.

Electrochemical Cells

Electromotive Force of a Cell

An electrochemical cell has two electrodes immersed in an electrolyte solution. Daniell cell is an electrochemical cell. It has got a Zinc electrode in a solution of $ZnSO_4$ in one compartment and a copper electrode in a solution of copper sulphate is the other compartment. These compartments are known as the half cell of the electrochemical cell. These are separated by a porous diaphragm. This porous diaphragm allows electric contact between the solutions. But, it does not permit excessive mixing of the two solutions.

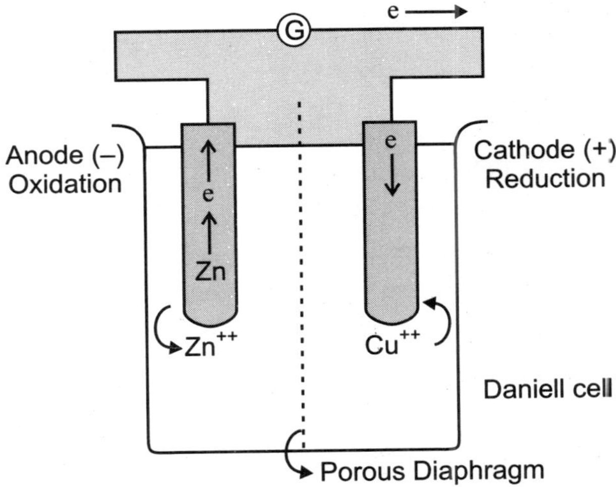

Zn^{2+} and SO_4^- ions diffuse through this porous diaphragm in opposite directions in order to maintain electroneutrality in each half cell as the reaction takes place.

Zinc has greater tendency to lose electrons as compared to copper. So spontaneous reaction occurs when the two half cells are connected by an external wire.

Atoms of the Zn electrode each solution as Zn^{2+} ions. It leaves electrons behind on the electrode. The electrons pass from this negatively charged electrode or anode via the external wire to the copper electrode. At cathode, copper ions from the solution take on electrons and they deposit copper atoms at the electrode surface. So, cathode loses electrons to the solution so it positively charged. So, here oxidation of Zn metal at the Zn electrode takes place and copper ions are reduced at the copper electrode.

The half reactions are expressed as:

Anode reaction (oxidation):

$$Zn = Zn^{2+} + 2e^{-} \; E_{left} \quad (1)$$

Cathode reaction (reduction):

$$Cu^{2+} + 2e^{-} = Cu \; E_{right}$$

Each half reaction shows the change occurring at a single electrode. Two half reactions are added together to express the overall cell reaction:

$$Zn + Cu^{2+} = Zn^{2+} + Cu$$

$$E_{cell} = E_{left} + E_{right}$$

The individual electrode potential are E_{left} and E_{right}. This occur at the junction between each electrode and its surrounding solution. The sum of the two electrode potentials is E_{cell}. This is the electromotive force (emf) or voltage of the cell. Emf is the voltage of the complete cell. Potential refers to the voltage from an electrode.

In order to summarise it:

Electrons are given upto the external circuit at the left electrode (anode) and accepted from the external circuit at the right electrode (cathode).

Measuring the Electromotive Force of Cells

A voltameter can draw a measurable amount of current from a circuit. So, the voltage determined becomes dependent on the resistance of the cell to current flow. According to Ohm's law E = IR. A potentiometer helps in measuring voltage by opposing the emf of a cell with an applied potential when no current is being drawn through the external circuit. It balances one current flow against another without producing changes in potential due to cell resistance.

Electrode potentials or half cell potentials are responsible for the emf of the cell. One can measure electrode potentials with respect to a reference electrode. For this purpose hydrogen electrode is used which is the reference electrode. This is assigned an arbitrary value of zero in the standard state. If the potential of the reference electrode is known, the potential of unknown electrode can be obtained as a difference. The measured emf is generally called as reduction potential. So unknown electrode is cathode of the cell. The relative ability of the electrode to accept electrons is measured against a reference electrode.

$$E_{cell} = E_{ref.} + E_{unknown\ electrode}$$

The potentials can be determined under standard conditions, i.e., 25°C and 1 atm. pressure. Then standard reduction potential becomes:

$$E^{\circ}_{cell} = E^{\circ}_{reference} + E^{\circ}_{unknown\ electrode}$$

Nernst Equation

Any half cell reaction is written as a reduction. That is, here an acceptance of electrons by the reactants to form products take place.

$$\underset{\text{Reactants}}{\alpha_{(Ox.)} + ne^-} \rightleftharpoons \underset{\text{Products}}{\beta_{(Red.)}}$$

α moles of oxidized species in the half cell is reduced by n electrons to form β moles of reduced species (Reduction) in the half cell.

The change in free energy for such a half cell reduction is:

$$\Delta F = \Delta F^{\circ} + RT\, I_n \frac{a_{(Red.)}\,\beta}{a_{(Ox.)}\,\alpha}$$

Now, – nFE is substituted for ΔF and – nFE° is substituted for ΔF°

$$-nFE = -nFE^{\circ} + RT\, I_n \frac{a_{(Red.)}\,\beta}{a_{(Ox.)}\,\alpha}$$

$$E = E^\circ - \frac{RT}{nF} I_n \frac{a_{(Red.)}\beta}{a_{(Ox.)}\alpha} \quad \text{(This is Nernst equation)}$$

Nernst equation is used to calculate either an individual electrode potential or a cell emf from a known E° at a specified temperature T. The reaction involves *n* electrons at specified activities of the reactants and products.

At 25°C, $$E = E^\circ - \frac{0.0592}{n} \log \frac{a_{products}}{a_{reactant}}$$

OXIDATION REDUCTION CURVES

In oxidimetric titration ions involved in the reaction or concentrate of the substances change continuously. So the oxidation potential of the solution (E) also changes continuously as the solution pH changes continuously during titration by the process of neutralization. When oxidation potential is plotted corresponding to different points in the titration, a titration curve is obtained which is similar to the curves for the neutralization method.

Example: The curve for titration of a ferrous iron salt with permanganate is acid solution is plotted. The ionic equation is written below:

$$MnO_4^- + 5Fe^{2+} + 8H^+ \rightleftharpoons Mn^{2+} + 5Fe^{3+} + 4H_2O$$

As the above reaction is reversible, the solution always contains both the original ions and the ions formed during the reaction. So it can be concluded that at any stage in the titration, the solution always contains two redox systems. Fe^{3+}/Fe^{2+} and MnO_4^-/Mn^{2+}.

So oxidation potential of the solution (E) is:

$$E = 0.77 + \frac{0.058}{1} \log \frac{[Fe^{3+}]}{[Fe^{2+}]} \quad ...(1)$$

$$E = 1.51 + \frac{0.058}{5} \log \frac{[MnO_4^-][H^+]^8}{[Mn^{2+}]} \quad ...(2)$$

Here equation (1) is more convenient to use even though both equations give the same result. So long as not all the ferrous iron has been converted and is easy to calculate the Fe^{3+} and Fe^{2+} concentrate at any point in the titration. The concentration of the MnO_4^- which is unconverted due to the reversibility of the reaction are much difficult to calculate.

If permanganate is in excess quantity then it is easy to calculate the concentrates of MnO_4^- and Mn^{2+} ions in solution and then is such case it becomes much more difficult to calculate the concentrate of the remaining Fe^{2+} ions. In such case equation (2) is to be used.

Here the oxidation potential of the solution is calculated when 50 ml of $KMnO_4$ solution is added to 100 ml of $FeSO_4$ solution of same normality. Here only 50% of the Fe^{2+} ions contained in 100 ml of the original solution is converted to Fe^{2+} ions.

$$\therefore \quad E = 0.77 + \frac{0.058}{1} \log \frac{50}{50} = 0.77 \text{ V}$$

The titration curves of those cases where 0.1 ml deficiency and 0.1 ml excess of $KMnO_4$ are considered. These points determine the magnitude of the break of potential at the equivalence point.

Example: 99.9 ml of $KMnO_4$ solution is added or 0.1 ml less than is required by the reaction equation is present so 0.1 ml of Fe^{2+} remains unoxidised in solution and all the rest of the Fe^{2+}, which was contained in 99.9 ml of the original solution has been titrated, i.e., converted to Fe^{3+}. Therefore at this point

$$E = 0.77 + \frac{0.058}{1} \log \frac{99.9}{0.1} = 0.944 \text{ V}$$

When 100.1 ml of permanganate solution has been added; of this volume, 100 ml was consumed in the titration with Fe^{2+} ions so that MnO_4^- is reduced to Mn^{2+}. The amount of permanganate contained in the added excess, i.e., 0.1 ml of solution remains is the form of MnO_4^- ions. So, the ratio $[MnO_4^-] : [Mn^{2+}]$ at this point is 0.1 : 100.

$$E = 1.51 + \frac{0.08}{5}\log\frac{0.10\times[H^+]^8}{100}$$

$[H^+]$ concentrate in the solution is 1 g ion/lit.

$$\therefore \quad E = 1.51 + \frac{0.058}{5}\log 10^{-3} = 1.4751\ V$$

E is calculated at the equivalence point

$$E = 0.77 + 0.058\log\frac{[Fe^{3+}]}{[Fe^{2+}]}$$

$$5E = 5\times 1.51 + 0.058\log\frac{[MnO_4^-]}{[Fe^{2+}][Mn^{2+}]}$$

$$6E = 0.77 + 5\times 1.51 + 0.058\log\frac{[Fe^{3+}][MnO_4^-]}{[Fe^{2+}][Mn^{2+}]} \quad ...(3)$$

Equation (2) is multiplied by 5 so that the coefficients of the logarithmic terms in equations (1) and (2) are equal.

At the equivalence point, the following reaction is observed:

$$5Fe^{2+} + MnO_4^- + 8H \rightleftharpoons 5Fe^{3+} + Mn^{2+} + 4H_2O$$

The amount of MnO_4^- ions added in the RK corresponds to the reaction equation written above. At equilibrium there must be $5Fe^{2+}$ ions for each MnO_4^- ion remaining in solution. At equivalence point the molar concentrate of Fe^{2+} ions is five times the concentrate of MnO_4^- ions, i.e.,

$$[Fe^{2+}] = 5[MnO_4^-]$$

At equivalence point

$$[Fe^{3+}] = 5[Mn^{2+}]$$

$\therefore$ Dividing the equations we get:

$$\frac{[Fe^{3+}]}{[Fe^{2+}]} = \frac{[Mn^{2+}]}{[MnO_4^-]} \text{ and } \frac{[Fe^{3+}][MnO_4^-]}{[Fe^{2+}][Mn^{2+}]} = 1$$

$$\because \quad \log 1 = 0$$

$$\therefore \quad 6E = 0.77 + 5 \times 1.51$$

$$E = \frac{0.77 + 5 \times 1.51}{6} = 1.387 \text{ V}$$

If the standard potential of the systems as per the oxidizing and reducing agents are taken as E_o' and E_o'', and their stoichiometric coefficients are a and b then the oxidation potential of the solution at the equivalence point is

$$E = \frac{bE_o' + aE_o''}{a + b}$$

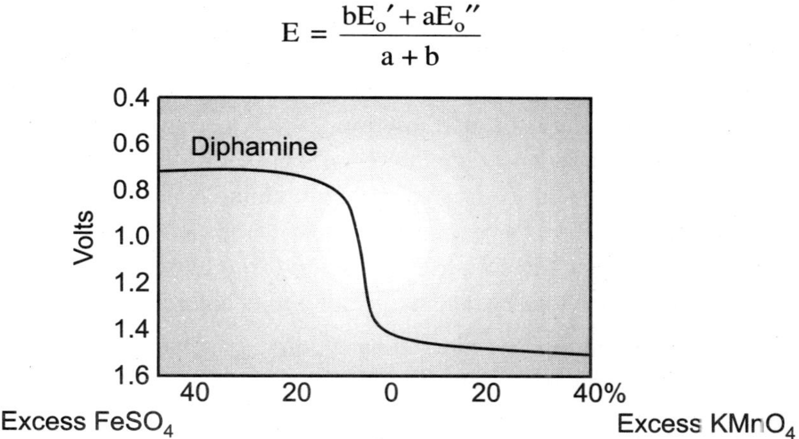

Curve for titration of $FeSO_4$ solution with permanganate at $[H^+] = 1$.

Here again there is an abrupt change of potential near the equivalence point. The curve is very flat in the remaining regions. This means E changes very slowly during the titration.

Oxidimetric titration curves are independent of dilution. This is due to the fact that the Nernst equation contains the ratio of the concentration of the oxidized and reduced form which does not change with dilution.

Indicators used in Oxidation-Reduction Methods

It is possible to do titration without indicator if the colour of the titrating solution undergoes a sharp changes as a result of the reaction.

Titration is possible without an indicator, e.g., when various reducing agents are oxidized by permanganate in acid solution. Here the purple-violet colour of the MnO_4^- ion disappears due to reduction to the almost colourless Mn^{2+} ion. When all the reducing agent gets titrated in this process, a single excess drop of permanganate makes the entire solution pink.

Reducing agents can also be titrated by iodine solution without using any indicator. The dark brown colour of iodine disappears due to the reduction of I_2 to I^- ions. Since the colour of I_2 solution is not very deep so it is better to use an indicator, i.e., starch solution, which gives an intense blue colour with a very small amounts of free iodine. Starch is used because of its ability to form a blue adsorption compound with iodine and is unrelated to the oxidizing properties of I_2.

Redox indicators are the indicators which change colour when the oxidation potential of the titrated solution reaches a definite value. Such colour changes do not depend on the specific properties of the oxidizing or reducing agents used. *Example*, Diphenyl-amine $NH(C_6H_5)_2$ is used in qualitative analysis as a reagent for the NO_3^- ion. NO_3^- ion oxidizes diphenylamine (which is colourless in solution) to another compound (diphenylbenzidine violet) which has a blue-violet colour.

Diphenylamine is also oxidized by oxidizing agents like $K_2Cr_2O_7$, $KMnO_4$, $KClO_3$ and KNO_2 etc. So Diphenylamine is a reagent for a definite oxidation potential.

Therefore, redox indicators are substances which can be reversibly oxidized or reduced, with different colours in the oxidized and reduced forms.

Example: $Ind._{Ox.} + ne \rightleftharpoons Ind._{Red.}$

A system consisting of $Ind_{Ox.}$ and $Ind_{Red.}$ is a redox system. Nernst equation to this case gives:

$$E = E_o + \frac{0.058}{n} \log \frac{[Ind._{Ox.}]}{[Ind._{Red.}]}$$

E_o = Std. oxidation potential of the system, i.e., potential of the situation.

When, $[Ind._{Ox.}] = [Ind._{Red.}]$

If 1-2 drops of a solution of some redox indicator is added to a solution of a reducing (or oxidizing) agent, then the concentration of the oxidized and reduced forms of the indicator will be in a ratio as per the oxidation potential of the solution. So the solution obtains colour according to that ratio. If this solution is titrated with a reducing or an oxidizing agent, then the oxidation potential E also changes and $[Ind._{Ox.}]/[Ind._{Red.}]$ ratio too changes accordingly.

The range in which the indicator changes its colour must be within the limits of the sharp change of potential on the titration curve so that the colour change of a redox indicator must be sharp. Indicator error in titration is small.

Redox Indicators

Indicator	$Ind._{Ox.}$	$Ind._{Red.}$
Neutral Red	Red	Colourless
Methylene blue	Greenish-blue	Colourless
Diphenylamine	Blue-violet	Colourless

Titrations Involving $KMnO_4$

Principle

The permanganate method of titration is based on the principle of reactions of oxidation by the permaganate ion. Oxidation occurs in acid or in alkaline (or neutral) solution.

$KMnO_4$ acts as an oxidizing agents in acid solution. Here the septivalent manganese is reduced to Mn^{++} cations and a manganese salt of the acid used is formed.

Example: Here $FeSO_4$ is the reducing agent. If $FeSO_4$ is oxidized in the presence of H_2SO_4, the reaction is shown below:

$$10FeSO_4 + 2KMnO_4 + 8H_2SO_4 = 5Fe_2(SO_4)_3 + 2MnSO_4 + K_2SO_4 + 8H_2O$$

In ionic form,

$$5Fe^{2+} + MnO_4^- + 8H^+ = 5Fe^{3+} + Mn^{2+} + 4H_2O$$

The valence of manganese decreases by 5 and it shows that the $KMnO_4$ molecule gains 5 electrons. The following equation shows it

$$MnO_4^- + 8H^+ + 5e = Mn^{2+} + 4H_2O$$

So, in this case, the gram-equivalent of

$$KMnO_4 = \frac{158.03}{5} = 31.61 \text{ g}$$

Oxidation in alkaline or neutral solution causes septivalent manganese to get reduced to quadrivalent manganese with the formation of MnO_2. MnO_2 is formed in the form of a brown ppt.

Example: $Cr_2(SO_4)_3 + 2KMnO_4 + 8KOH = 2K_2CrO_4 + \downarrow 2MnO_2 + 2K_2SO_4 + 4H_2O$

The change which takes place in MnO_4^- ion is shown by the equation:

$$MnO_4^- + 4H^+ + 3e = MnO_2 + 2H_2O$$

Here the gram equivalent of $KMnO_4$ is

$$= \frac{158.03}{3} = 52.68 \text{ g}$$

If two types of titration are compared then the standard oxidation potential of the MnO_4^-/Mn^{++} system (+ 1.51 V) is higher than that of: MnO_4^-/MnO_2 (+ 0.59 V). The oxidizing activity of permanganate is high in acid solution as compared to that of alkaline solution.

Colourless Mn^{2+} ions remain in solution in titration in acid solution but titration in alkaline or neutral solution results in the formation of a dark brown ppt. of MnO_2 which creates difficulty in establishing the equivalent point during titration. That's why, oxidation with permanganate in acid solution is used in volumetric analysis.

DETERMINATION OF FERROUS IRON, H_2O_2 AND NITRITES

Oxidations with Cerium (IV) Sulphate Solution

Cerium (IV) sulphate is an oxidizing agent. It can be used in acid solution in concentrate of 0.5 M or higher concentrations, as the solution is neutralized to cerium (IV) hydroxide [hydrated cerium (IV) oxide] or basic salts ppt. The solution has deep yellow colour. In hot solutions which are not too dilute, the end point is detected without an indicator. This procedure needs a blank determination. It is preferable to add an indicator.

Advantages of Cerium (IV) Sulphate as are standard oxidising agent are:

(i) Cerium (IV) sulphate solutions are stable over prolonged periods.

(ii) Cerium (IV) solutions in 0.1 M solution are not too dense coloured to obstruct vision while reading in burette.

(iii) In the reaction of cerium (IV) salts in acid solution with reducing agents, the following change takes place

$$Ce^{4+} + e \rightleftharpoons Ce^{3+}$$

Solutions of cerium (IV) sulphate in dilute H_2SO_4 are stable even at boiling temperature of the system.

Hydrochloric acid solutions of the salt are unstable. This is because reduction to cerium (III) by the acid occurs with liberation of chlorine.

$$2Ce^{4+} + 2Cl^- = 2Ce^{3+} + Cl_2$$

The above reaction occurs on boiling so HCl cannot be used in oxidations which needs boiling with excess of cerium (IV) sulphate in acid solution. So in such cases H_2SO_4 is used.

Preparation of 0.1 N Cerric ammonium sulphate solution (CAS solution):

$Ce(SO_4)_2$, $2(NH_4)_2SO_4 \cdot 2H_2O$ (63.26 g in 1000 ml). Here 66 g of CAS is dissolved in a mixture of 30 ml of H_2SO_4 and 500 ml of water. This is cooled and filtered. Then vol. is made upto 1000 ml with water.

Std. of 0.1 N CAS (Using Arsenic Trioxide)

0.2 g of Arsenic trioxide is (dried at 105°C for 1 hour) taken. This is transferred to 500 ml conical flask. To this 25 ml of 8% w/v solution of NaOH and 100 ml of water is added. To this mixture 30 ml of dilute H_2SO_4, 0.15 ml of osmic acid solution and 0.1 ml of ferroin sulphate solution is added as indicator. This is titrated against 0.1 N CAS until pink colour becomes pale blue.

Each 4.946 mg of Arsenic trioxide is equivalent to 1 ml of 0.1 N CAS or 0.06326 g of CAS.

Std. of 0.1 N CAS [Using FAS (Ferrous Ammonium Sulphate)]

39.22 g of ferrous ammonium sulphate is dissolved in water upto 1000 ml. 20 ml of this solution is taken by means of pipette into a conical flask. To this 20 ml of 1 N H_2SO_4 is added and then 1-2 drops of ferrion sulphate solution as indicator. The contents of the flask is titrated against 0.1 N CAS solution until the colour becomes pale blue.

Application of Redox Titration Using CAS

(i) Ascorbic acid tablets

(ii) Ferrous fumarate tablets

(iii) Ferrous gluconate tablets

(iv) Chlorpromazine tablets

(v) Tocopheryl acetate.

POTASSIUM IODATE TITRATIONS

Potassium iodate is a strong oxidizing agent. It reacts quantitatively with both iodates and iodine. Iodate titration is carried out in the presence of alcohol, saturated organic acids and other kinds of organic matter.

Example: Determination of the percentage of KI by titration with potassium iodate.

The sample, around 0.5 g, is dissolved in 50 ml water. To this concentration HCl (60 ml) is added and titrated against 0.05 M potassium iodate solution. The solution gets brown as the titration occurs due to the liberation of iodine. The solution then gets a lighter colour as titration is continued due to the iodine monochloride which is formed during the process. The solution then turns pale yellow. Then 1 ml of amaranth solution is added and titration is continued. Then red colour becomes pale yellow. Amaranth is an azo dye. It is oxidized by excess titrant at the end point to a colourless derivative. Instead of Amaranth, chloroform can also be used as indicator. Chloroform is not soluble in aqueous solution and gives a violet coloured solution in the presence of iodine. Here, vigorous shaking is needed because end point ensures equilibrium between the indicator and titration solutions. End point is reached when chloroform solution becomes colourless.

Principle

If the concentrate of HCl does not exceed 1 M, the reaction between potassium iodate and KI stops when the iodate gets reduced to free iodine.

$$IO_3^- + 5I^- + 6H^+ \longrightarrow 3I_2 + 3H_2O \quad ...(1)$$

If more concentrate HCl (i.e., greater than 4 M) is present, then iodine produced in the reaction is oxidized by iodate to iodine cation, I^+. The high concentrate of chloride ion forms iodine monochloride. Iodine monochloride is stabilized from getting hydrolysed by HCl present.

$$2[I_2 \longrightarrow 2I^+ + 2e]$$

$$IO_3^- + 6H^+ + 4e \longrightarrow 3H_2O + I^+$$

$$5I^+ + 5Cl^- = 5I\,Cl$$

∴ The reaction is written as:

$$KIO_3 + 2I_2 + 6HCl \longrightarrow KCl + 5ICl + 3H_2O \quad ...(2)$$

By combining equations (1) and (2) the complete reaction between KIO_3 and KI in the presence of 4M HCl is expressed as:

$$KIO_3 + 2KI_2 + 6HCl \longrightarrow 3KCl + 3ICl + 3H_2O_2$$

$$2 \times 166 \text{ g KI} \equiv 1000 \text{ ml M } KIO_3$$

∴ $1 \text{ ml } 0.05 \text{ M } KIO_3 \cong 0.0166 \text{ g KI}.$

Standardization of Potassium Iodate Solution

Since potassium iodate is purchased in a high state of purity of around 99.9% so a standard solution can be prepared by direct weighing.

In general, the following methods are used for standardization:

(i) To a definite amount of potassium iodate solution, excess of KI and dilute HCl is added and liberated iodine is titrated against std. sod. thiosulphate solution.

(ii) Pure KI can be used and determination is done as described under the determination of KI.

POTASSIUM BROMATE

Oxidations with Potassium Bromate:

Principle

Potassium bromate is an oxidizing agent which is reduced to bromide

$$BrO_3^- + 6H^+ + 6e \rightleftharpoons Br^- + 3H_2O$$

Its molecular mass is 167. A 0.02 M solution has 3.34 g/lit of potassium bromate. When the titration is complete free bromine appears:

$$BrO_3^- + 5Br^- + 6H^+ = 3Br_2 + 3H_2O$$

The presence of free bromine and hence the end point is detected by its yellow colour. Indicators like methyl orange, Me red, naphthalene black 12B, xylidine ponceau and fuchsine are also used. The above mentioned indicators have their usual colour in acid solution but are destroyed by the first excess of bromine. Direct titration with bromate solution in the presence of indicators which are irreversible dyestuff are done in HCl solution. The concentrate of HCl must be within 1.5-2 M. At the end of titration, some chlorine may appear by the reaction:

$$10Cl^- + 2BrO_3^- + 12H^+ = 5Cl_2 + Br_2 + 6H_2O$$

This Bleaches the Indicator

The titration must be done slowly so that the indicator change which takes time can be readily detected. At the end point, if the indicator is irreversibly destroyed and the solution becomes colourless and if the fading of the indicator is confused with the equivalence point, another drop of indicator is to be added. This is because if the indicator has faded the additional drop will colour the solution. Once the end-point is reached, the additional drop of indicator will be destroyed by the slight excess of bromate present in the solution.

It reversible redox indicators are added in the determination of arsenic (III) and antimony (II), then the procedure gets simplified. Examples of such indicators include 1-naphthoflavone and p-ethoxychrysoidine. When antimony (III) is titrated with bromate in the presence of the reversible indicators then a little of tartaric acid or KNa tartrate is added as this prevents hydrolysis at the lower acid concentration. End-point can be determined potentiometrically.

The following are the examples of determinations utilising direct titration with bromate solutions.

$$BrO_3^- + 3H_3ASO_3 \xrightarrow{HCl} Br^- + 3H_3ASO_4$$

$$2BrO_3^- + 3N_2H_4 \xrightarrow{HCl} Br^- + 3N_2 + 6H_2O$$

$$BrO_3^- + NH_2OH \xrightarrow{HCl} Br^- + NO_3^- + H^+ + H_2O$$

$$BrO_3^- + 6[Fe(CN)_6]^{4-} + 6H^+ \longrightarrow Br^- + 6[Fe(CN)_6]^{3-} + 3H_2O$$

Example: Determination of antimony in tartar emetic.

Tartar emetic is a basic tartrate of trivalent antimony. Its formula is $K(SbO)\ C_4H_4O_6$. When this solution is titrated with $KBrO_3$ solution in acidic condition, i.e., in the presence of HCl, the following reaction takes place:

$$3K(SbO)\ C_4H_4O_6 + KBrO_3 + 15HCl = 3SbCl_5 + 3KHC_4H_4O_6 + KBr + 6H_2O$$

Here each atom of trivalent antimony loses two electrons and gets oxidised to equivalent antimony.

Therefore, the gram-equivalent of antimony is:

$$g - Eq\ Sb = \frac{121.75}{2} = 60.88\ g$$

Procedure

4 g of tartar emetic is dissolved in 250 ml of water in a flask (volumetric). Then 25 ml of the solution is diluted to 100 ml with water in a conical flask. Add 15 ml of concentrate HCl and is heated to 70°C.

Then 2-3 drops of Me orange or Me red indicator is added. This is titrated against std. $KBrO_3$ solution. At the end of the titration when the colour of the solution gets fainter then a few drops of indicator is again added. Then titrated is continued until the colour changes sharply.

If the titration is repeated and the vol. of KBO_3 solution gets 0.5-1 ml less than the previous volume, then the solution is warmed again to 70°C and then only the indicator is added. Titration process must be slow until the indicator is decolorized. Then average result is taken.

Calculation

Calculation of antimony titre of the $KBrO_3$ solution is done from normality.

$$T_{KBrO_3/Sb} = \frac{N_{KBrO_3} \times 60.88}{1000}$$

Then the total amount of antimony in the sample is calculated, i.e., in 250 ml solution percentage is determined.

IODOMETRY

Principle

The iodometry is a method of volumetric analysis. It is based on Oxidation-Reduction process which involves interconversion of elemental iodine and I^- ions.

$$I_2 + 2e \rightleftharpoons 2I^-$$

Free iodine can take electrons from reducing agents. So, it is an oxidant. When it comes in contact with substances which gains electrons (i.e., oxidants), I^- ions readily donates electrons and acts as reducing agent. The standard oxidation potential of $I_2/2I^-$ system is + 0.54 V. So, in contrary to the oxidizing agents like $KMnO_4$ or $K_2Cr_2O_7$, I_2 is a weak oxidant. But I^- ions are more powerful reducing agents than Cr^{3+} or Mn^{2+} ions. There is a dual possibility of using the Oxidation-Reduction properties of the $I_2/2I^-$ system in volumetric analysis for determination of reducing agents by oxidation with iodine solution and for determination of oxidizing agents by reduction with I^- ions.

Both Types of Iodometric Titrations

Determination of Reducing Agents:

Sodium thiosulfate solution reacts with free iodine as follows:

$$2Na_2S_2O_3 + I_2 = 2NaI + \underset{\text{Sod. tetrathionate}}{Na_2S_4O_6}$$

Iodometric Reaction is written in Ionic form as

$$2S_2O_3^{2} + I_2 = 2I^- + S_4O_6^{2-}$$

Here $2S_2O_3^{2-}$ ions with four excess electrons are converted into a single $S_4O_6^{2-}$ ion with only 2 excess electrons. That is, two $S_2O_3^{2-}$ ions give two electrons to the I_2 molecule.

Structural form:

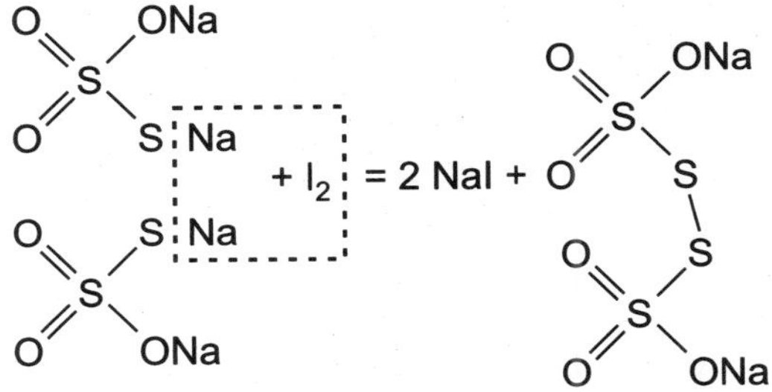

O ONa
S
O S Na
$+ I_2$ = 2 NaI + O ONa
O S Na S
S
O ONa

2 Molecules of $Na_2S_2O_3$ 1 Molecule of $Na_2S_4O_6$

When sodium thiosulfate solution is titrated against iodine solution, the dark brown colour of iodine disappears. When all the sodium thiosulphate gets oxidized then one excess drop of iodine solution makes the liquid pale yellow coloured. The colour due to iodine at the end point is faint so it makes determination of equivalence point hard. So starch solution is used as indicator. The latter forms an intense blue absorption compound with iodine. When one excess drop of iodine is added in the titration in the presence of starch solution, a permanent blue colour is obtained. Iodine solution is titrated with thiosulphate solution until one drop of thiosulphate decolorises the blue solution. In this case, starch solution must be added at the end of titration as at that time only a very little iodine remains and the solution being titrated has a pale yellow colour. It is because of starch is added earlier then iodine starch compound formed reacts slowly with thiosulphate so too much thiosulphate gets added.

Reducing agents are determined by titration with iodine solution. So for determination of oxidizing agents, reduction by I^- ions, KI solution is added for titration. But in this case it gets difficult to determine the equivalence point. When an oxidant like $K_2Cr_2O_7$ is titrated with KI solution then the end of the reaction is characterized by a cessation of iodine liberation. But, this point is not detected.

$$K_2Cr_2O_7 + 6KI + 14HCl = 3I_2 + 8KCl + 2CrCl_3 + 7H_2O$$

When starch is used as an indicator, it is easy to detect the moment when iodine appears in solution by formation of blue colour. When iodine disappears then the colour also disappears. But this does not state the instant when iodine formation ceases. So, an indirect substitution method is used. Here a mixture of KI and acid solution taken in an excess quantity. Then an exact volume of oxidant to be determined is added from a pipette.

Example: $K_2Cr_2O_7$ solution.

For the reaction to get completed, the solution is left to stand for 5 minutes. Then the liberated iodine is titrated against thiosulphate solution taken in a burette. The number of gram-equivalents of thiosulphate taken is equal to the number of gram-equivalents of the oxidizing agent ($K_2Cr_2O_7$). Although $K_2Cr_2O_7$ and $Na_2S_2O_3$ do not react directly with each other, then also their respective amounts are equivalent.

Formula used for calculation:

$$V_{K_2Cr_2O_7} N_{K_2Cr_2O_7} = V_{Na_2S_2O_3} N_{Na_2S_2O_3}$$

Iodometric determination of oxidizing agents is written as:

(a) KI + acid (excess in flask) + oxidant to be determined is weighed or pipetted $\longrightarrow$ liberation of I_2 on standing.

(b) $I_2 + 2Na_2S_2O_3 = 2NaI + Na_2S_4O_6$ (This is titration of iodine with thiosulphate).

IODIMETRY AND IODOMETRY

Iodimetry means titration with standard solution of iodine. Iodometry deals with those titrations where iodine is liberated in chemical reaction. This analytical method depends on inter-conversion of elemental I_2 and iodide ion.

$$I_2 + 2e \longrightarrow 2I^-$$

Free iodine is liberated due to oxidation of KI in a acidic solution. The liberated iodine is titrated with standard solution of sodium thiosulphate. Free iodine gets converted to I^- ion by reducing agent. So, the method of iodometry is used for quantitative determination of oxidizing and reducing agents. Due to the great sensitivity, iodometry is the most accurate method for determination of the % of oxidizing and reducing agents.

Conditions for Iodometric Determination

(i) The potential of $I_2/2I^-$ system is not high so, iodometric reactions are reversible and do not give end-point unless suitable conditions are provided.

(ii) Iodine is volatile in nature so titration is conducted in cold condition. Activity of starch decreases with rise in temperature.

(iii) Solubility of iodine in water is least so KI must be used.

(iv) Even though large amounts of KI and acid are used, the rate of reaction between oxidant and I^- ions is to slow. So enough time must be given before titration.

(v) The reaction mixture is kept in dark as light accelerates the side reactions which causes oxidation of I^- ions to I_2 by atm, oxygen.

$$4I^- + 4H^+ + O_2 \longrightarrow I_2 + 2H_2O$$

(vi) Iodometric titration cannot be performed in strongly alkaline solution as it forms hypoiodide.

$$2NaOH + I_2 \longrightarrow NaOI + NaI + H_2O$$

Hypoiodide is a strong oxidizing agent.

If the reaction results in the formation of H^+ ions these ions must be removed to enable the reaction to proceed to completion.

$$HCO_3^- + H^+ \longrightarrow H_2CO_3 \longrightarrow H_2O + CO_2\uparrow$$

Preparation of Sodium Thiosulphate Solution:

Preparation of 0.1 N sodium thiosulphate solution: 25 g of sodium thiosulphate is weighed and dissolved in freshly boiled and cooled distilled water. Then the volume is made upto 1000 ml in volumetric flask. The redox process that takes place when $Na_2S_2O_3$ reacts with I_2 is shown below:

$$2Na_2S_2O_3 + I_2 \longrightarrow NaO{-}S(=O)_2{-}S{=}S{-}S(=O)_2{-}ONa + 2NaI$$

$$2S_2O_3^{2-} - 2e \longrightarrow S_4O_6^{2-}$$

$$I_2 + 2e \longrightarrow 2I^-$$

Two molecules of thiosulphate loose 2 electrons so gram equivalent of sodium thiosulphate = 1 mole.

Standardization of Sodium Thiosulphate Solution

1. With Potassium Dichromate

Potassium dichromate is an oxidizing agent and is a primary standard. For standardization of sodium thiosulphate, a known quantity of potassium dichromate is first dissolved in water. This is then acidified with HCl and excess of KI is added potassium dichromate oxidizes KI to iodine. The liberated iodine is then titrated against sodium thiosulphate. Starch solution is used as indicator and titration is continued till pale green colour is obtained.

The reactions are shown below:

$$K_2Cr_2O_7 + 6KI + 7H_2SO_4 \longrightarrow Cr_2(SO_4)_3 + 3I_2 + 4K_2SO_4 + 7H_2O$$

$$Cr_2O_7^{2-} + 14H^+ + 6e \longrightarrow 2Cr^{3+} + 7H_2O$$

$$6I^- - e \longrightarrow 3I_2$$

$$\therefore \text{ Equivalent wt. of } K_2Cr_2O_7 = \frac{\text{Mol. wt.}}{7} = 49.03.$$

2. With Potassium Iodate

Potassium iodate is a primary standard. It reacts with potassium iodide in acid solution to liberate iodine. The liberated iodine is titrated against sodium thiosulphate.

$$KIO_3 + 5KI + 6HCl \longrightarrow 6KCl + 3I_2 + 3H_2O$$

Here potassium iodate is weight and dissolved in cold distilled water. Add KI and sulphuric acid to it. The liberated iodine is titrated against sodium thiosulphate solution till pale yellow colour is obtained. Starch solution is added and titration is continued to get colourless solution.

Preparation of Iodine Solution

Commercial iodine is contaminated. So it is purified by sublimation. Iodine is very slightly soluble in water. So it is dissolved in KI solution. Iodine dissolves in KI solution due to formation of triodide ions.

$$I_2 + I^- \longrightarrow I_3^-$$

$$I_2 + 2e \longrightarrow 2I^-$$

$$\text{Equivalent wt.} = \frac{126.5}{1}.$$

Preparation of 0.1 N Iodine Solution

20 g of Iodine is dissolved in 30-40 ml water in 1 litre flask. Add 12.7 g of resublimed iodine to this KI solution. This is shaken well to dissolve iodine. Volume is made upto the mark with distilled water. This solution is stored in glass stoppered bottled in dark.

Standardization of Iodine

1. Standardization with Arsenious Trioxide Solution

2.5 g of powdered arsenious trioxide is dissolved in sodium hydroxide solution. This is diluted to 200 ml. This solution is neutralized with HCl. Then pure sodium bicarbonate is added and when the salt gets dissolved then the volume is made upto 500 ml with water. Then fixed volume of arsenious trioxide is taken in conical flask and is titrated against iodine solution. End point is permanent pale stram colour.

2. Standardization with Sodium Thiosulphate

Iodine solution is pipetted out. This is titrated against sodium thiosulphate solution till pale yellow colour is obtained. Starch solution is added and titration is continued till the solution becomes colourless.

Detection of End-point

Iodine solution has intense yellow to brown colour. One drop of 0.1 N iodine solution gives pale yellow colour to 100 ml of water. So in colourless solutions, it can act as its own indicator. Test becomes sensitive by using starch solution as indicator. Starch reacts with iodine to form an intense blue coloured complex. This complex is visible at very low concentrate of iodine colour sensitivity decreases upon addition of solvent like ethanol. Starch gets hydrolysed in acidic medium so it can not be used. CCl_4 or $CHCl_3$ can be used in certain reactions instead of starch to detect end point. The liberated iodine dissolves in those solvents due to high solubility. The end point is marked by disappearance of colour from organic layer. End-point can also be determined potentiometrically.

TITANOUS CHLORIDE

Titanous chloride is a strong reducing agent. It works on the principle of redox titration.

Preparation of 0.1 N Titanous Chloride

10.3 ml of titanous chloride is added to 100 ml of HCl. Then it is diluted to 1000 ml with freshly boiled and cooled water. This is mixed well by stirring. Standardization of the solution is to be done before use.

Standardization of 0.1 N Titanous Chloride

30 ml of standardized 0.1 N ferric ammonium sulphate is taken in a flask. This is passed through a rapid stream of CO_2 until all air gets removed. Then titanous chloride is added from burette in an atmosphere

of carbon dioxide until the end point arrives. Then 5 ml of ammonium thiocyanate solution is added and titration is continued until the solution becomes colourless.

Each ml of 0.1 N ferric amm. sulphate is equivalent to 0.01543 g of $TiCl_3$.

Application

Titanous chloride is used in the estimation of ferric salts, azo dyes nitro compounds, nitroso compounds and quinones.

Types of Titration

1. Direct Titration

Quinones, azo dyes and ferric salts are assayed by this technique. When coloured substances are titrated then indicators are not needed.

Example: Titration of Methylene blue with 0.1 N titanous chloride. Here indicator is not used. Disappearance of blue colour is the end-point of titration. Indigocarmine and nitranilic acid are assayed by direct titration.

2. Back Titration

Back titration method is applied in cases where compounds are not readily reduced. Here a known excess of 0.1 N titanous chloride is added to the sample for reaction. The excess of 0.1 N titanous chloride is back titrated with 0.1 N ferric ammonium sulphate using ammonium thiocyanate is indicator.

Example: Chloramphenicol, Metronidazole, Dyes like brilliant green and crystal violet. Then drugs with nitro group and nitroso compounds are assayed by this technique.

Direct Titration with Iodine

Direct titration with iodine makes use of oxidizing power of iodine in aqueous solution.

$$I_2 + 2e \longrightarrow 21$$

$$I_2 \equiv 2I^- \equiv 2e$$

$$2 \times 126.9 \text{ g } I_2 \equiv 1000 \text{ ml M} = 2000 \text{ ml N}$$

$$\therefore \quad 12.69 \text{ g } I_2 \equiv 1000 \text{ ml } 0.05 \text{ M solution}$$

1 M and 2 N solutions contain same concentrate of I. As iodine is practically insoluble in water, so it is dissolved in KI to form KI_3. The latter behaves in solution as free iodine.

Iodine is volatile in nature so standard solutions must be stored in tightly stoppered (glass) bottles.

Standardization of approximately 0.5 M iodine solution by arsenic trioxide:

The standardization procedure depends upon the following reactions:

$$As_2O_3 + 2H_2O \longrightarrow As_2O_5 + 4H^+ + 4e$$

$$I_2 + 2e \equiv 2I^-$$

$$\therefore \quad As_2O_3 \equiv 2I_2$$

$$\therefore \quad 197.8 \text{ g } As_2O_3 \equiv 2000 \text{ ml M}$$

$$\therefore \quad 0.0496 \text{ g } As_2O_3 \equiv 100 \text{ ml } 0.05 \text{ M iodine}$$

Since hydriodic acid has a strong reducing properties so oxidation with iodine is a reversible reaction.

$$As_2O_3 + 2O_2 + 2H_2O \rightleftharpoons As_2O_5 + 4H^+ + 4I^-$$

The reaction goes to right hand side, i.e., to As_2O_5 by removal of HI with $NaHCO_3$.

Here sodium bicarbonate is used and not NaOH or Na_2CO_3 as they cannot remove HI because they reaction with iodine as per the following reactions:

$$6NaOH + 3I_2 \longrightarrow 5NaI + NaIO_3 + 3H_2O$$

$$3Na_2CO_3 + 3I_2 \longrightarrow 5NaI + NaIO_3 + 3CO_2$$

In this standardization procedure, after the addition of HCl, testing of acidity is done with a little $NaHCO_3$ when effervescence should occur. This acidification is needed to remove the free NaOH which would react with iodine. $NaHCO_3$ is added to remove the excess acid.

Applications

1. Estimation of Ascorbic Acid (% of $C_6H_8O_6$)

The assay depends upon the quantitative oxidation of ascorbic acid to dehydroascorbic acid with iodine acid solution.

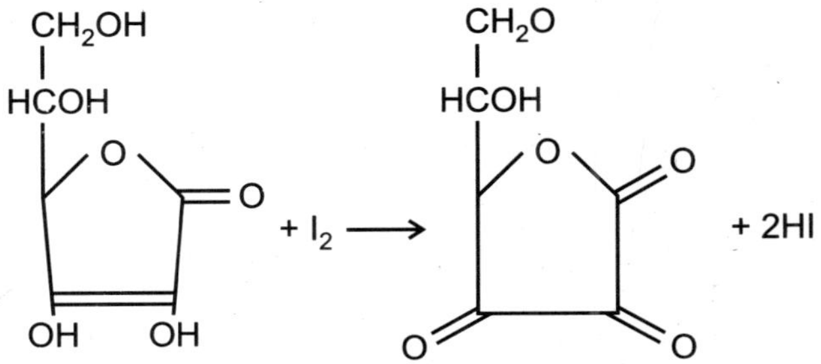

$$\text{Ascorbic acid (CH}_2\text{OH–HCOH–lactone ring with enediol OH, OH)} + I_2 \longrightarrow \text{Dehydroascorbic acid (CH}_2\text{O–HCOH–lactone ring with two C=O)} + 2HI$$

$\therefore \quad C_6H_8O_6 \equiv I_2$

$\therefore \quad 176.1 \text{ g } C_6H_8O_6 = 1000 \text{ ml M Iodine}$

0.2 g of ascorbic acid is taken in a conical flask. To this 80 ml distilled water is added and 10 ml of M sulfuric acid. This is titrated against 0.05 M iodine solution using starch solution as indicator.

2. To determine the % w/w of Dimercaprol

The reaction depends on the oxidation of thiol groups with iodine. It is not a reversible reaction.

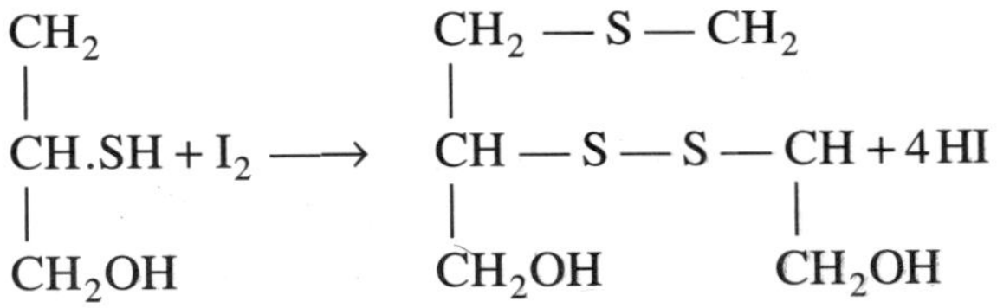

$$\begin{array}{l} CH_2 \\ | \\ CH.SH + I_2 \longrightarrow \\ | \\ CH_2OH \end{array} \quad \begin{array}{l} CH_2 - S - CH_2 \\ | \\ CH - S - S - CH + 4HI \\ | \qquad\qquad\quad | \\ CH_2OH \qquad CH_2OH \end{array}$$

0.2 g of sample is taken. To this 40 ml of 0.1 M HCl is added and titrated against 0.05 M iodine solution.

Official product: Dimercaprol Injection.

Applications of Iodometry and Iodimetry

Drug	Type	Titrant
Analgin	Iodimetry	Iodine
Analgin Tablets	Iodimetry	Iodine
Ascorbic acid	Iodimetry	Iodine
Soluble Aspirin Tablets	Iodometry	Sodium thiosulphate

Cont...

Cyclobarbitone Tablets	Iodimetry	Sodium thiosulphate
Cephalodrine	Iodimetry	Sodium thiosulphate
Cephalodrine Injection	Iodimetry	Sodium thiosulphate
Cetrimide	Iodimetry	KIO_3
Mephenezin	Iodometry	Sodium thiosulphate
Benzylin	Iodometry	Sodium thiosulphate
Thyroid	Iodometry	Sodium thiosulphate
Thyroid Tablets	Iodometry	Sodium thiosulphate

CHAPTER 4

NON-AQUEOUS TITRATIONS

Non-aqueous titration is the process by which the weakly acidic and weakly basic substances are titrated to get sharp end-point. This process is also used for those substances which are insoluble in water.

Substances which are either too weakly acidic or too weakly basic cannot give sharp end-points in aqueous solutions. Bronsted Lowry theory explains the reactions which occur during many non-aqueous titrations. As per Bronsted Lowry theory, an acid is a proton donor and base is a proton acceptor. So, a substance which dissociates to give a proton is an acid whereas a substance which tends to combine with a proton is base. When an acid such as HB dissociates, it yields a proton along with the conjugate base B of the acid.

$$\underset{\text{Acid}}{HB} \rightleftharpoons \underset{\text{Proton}}{H^+} + \underset{\text{Base}}{B^-}$$

Similarly, the base B combines with a proton to give the conjugate acid HB of the base. Every base has its conjugated acid and *vice versa*.

Example: $HCl \rightleftharpoons H^+ + Cl^-$

$$HNO_3 \rightleftharpoons H^+ + NO_3^-$$

$$HSO_4^- \rightleftharpoons H^+ + SO_4^{2-}$$

TYPES OF SOLVENTS

Solvents are classified as per their properties as follows:

1. Aprotic solvents
2. Protogenic solvents
3. Protophilic solvents
4. Amphiprotic solvents

Aprotic Solvents are Neutral in Nature

They are chemically inert substances such as toluene and chloroform. They do not favour ionization, i.e., they do not react with either acids or bases. They have low dielectric constant.

Example: Picric acid gives a colourless solution in toluene. The colour becomes yellow on adding aniline. This proves that picric acid is not dissociated in toluene solution. In the presence of aniline (which is a base) it functions as an acid – yellow colour develops due to the formation of picrate ion.

The reaction can be written as:

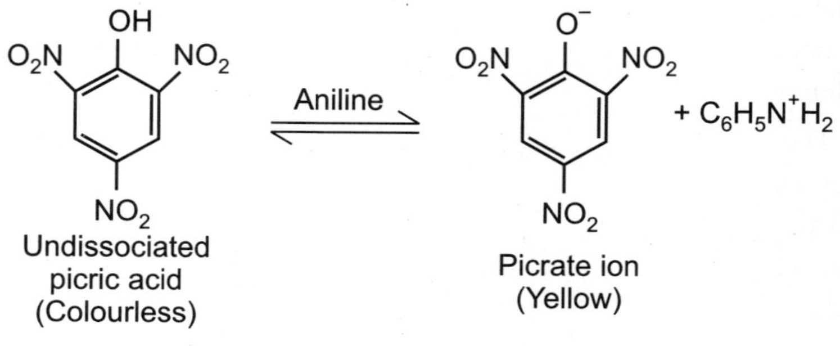

OH, O_2N, NO_2, NO_2 — Aniline ⇌ — O^-, O_2N, NO_2, NO_2 $+ C_6H_5N^+H_2$

Undissociated picric acid (Colourless)

Picrate ion (Yellow)

Aprotic solvents are added to ionizing solvents to depress solvolysis of the neutralization product. This sharpens the end-point.

Protogenic Solvents (Genic – Producing)

Protogenic solvents are acidic in nature. They yield protons.

Example: H_2SO_4, HCl, HNO_3.

Protophilic Solvents (Philic – Loving)

They are basic in nature and has the tendency to abstract proton from acids. So they yield solvated protons.

$$\underset{\text{Acid}}{HB} + \underset{\text{Basic}}{\text{Solvent}} \rightleftharpoons \underset{\text{Solvated proton}}{\text{Solution } H^+} + \underset{\text{Conjugated base of the acid}}{B^-}$$

Protophilic solvents are of two types:

1. Strongly basic solvent
2. Weakly basic solvent

A **strongly basic solvent** has stronger tendency to accept proton. Likewise, weakly basic solvent has less or weaker tendency to accept a proton.

A strongly basic solvent is also known as a levelling solvent (for weak and strong acids) as it can abstract a proton from any acid. It does not matter for it whether the acid is stronger or weak. This effect of strongly basic solvent is called as levelling effect since it does not make any difference between strong or weak acids.

A **weakly basic solvent** has weak or lesser tendency to accept proton. So, this solvent is also called as differentiating solvent. It is due to the fact that it can abstract proton from strongly acidic substances and not from weak acids. This effect is called as differentiating effect. Differentiating solvents are not useful in non-aqueous titrations.

Therefore, strongly acidic solvents are levelling solvents for weak bases and strong base. That is, strongly acidic solvents can donate proton to strong bases as well as weak bases equally. So, a strongly acidic solvent like perchloric acid in acetic acid is used in the titration of weak bases.

Amphiprotic Solvents

Such type of solvents have both protophilic and protogenic properties.

Example: Water, alcohols and acetic acid. They get dissociated slightly. Acetic acid is used as a solvent for titration of basic substances. Dissociation of acetic acid is shown the following equation:

$$CH_3COOH \rightleftharpoons H^+ + CH_3COO^-$$

Here acetic acid is functioning as a proton donor or an acid. When a strong acid like perchloric acid is dissolved in acetic acid, then acetic acid functions as a base and combines with protons donated by the perchloric acid to form an Onium ion.

The reactions are expressed as:

$$HClO_4 \rightleftharpoons H^+ + ClO_4^-$$

$$CH_3COOH + H^+ \rightleftharpoons \underset{\text{Onium ion}}{CH_3COOH_2^+}$$

Here the onium ion ($CH_3COOH_2^+$ ion) easily donates its proton to a base, a solution of perchloric acid in glacial acetic acid therefore acts as a strongly acidic solution.

When weak bases like pyridine are dissolved in acetic acid then equivalent amount of acetate ions are produced which have high tendency to accept protons. The reaction is shown below:

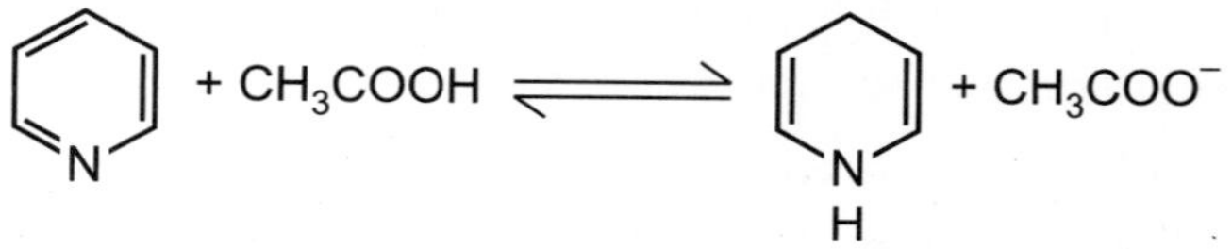

$$C_5H_5N \text{ (pyridine)} + CH_3COOH \rightleftharpoons C_5H_5NH^+ + CH_3COO^-$$

So, it is possible to titrate a solution of a weak base in acetic acid with $HClO_4$ on acetic acid and obtain a sharp end-point. This attempt is successful when titration in aqueous solutions are unsuccessful.

The series of reactions are given below:

$$HClO_4 + CH_3COOH \longrightarrow \underset{\text{(Onium ions)}}{CH_3COOH_2^+} + ClO_4^-$$

$$C_5H_5N + CH_3COOH \longrightarrow C_5H_5NH^+ + \underset{\text{(Acetate ion)}}{CH_3COO^-}$$

$$\underset{\text{(Burette)}}{CH_3COOH_2^+} + \underset{\text{(Conical flask)}}{CH_3COO^-} \longrightarrow 2CH_3COOH$$

∴ The net reaction is:

$$HClO_4 + C_5H_5N \longrightarrow C_5H_5NH^+ ClO_4^-$$

So, it can be concluded that the tendency of acid to donate proton is ↑ and the tendency of base to accept proton is ↑. This yields the sharp end-point in non-aqueous titrations.

The above noted theory forms the basis of non-aqueous titration of weak bases with perchloric acid.

Interference due to water in non-aqueous titrations:

$$H_2O \rightleftharpoons H^+ + OH^-$$

In the presence of weakly basic drug water (OH^-) acts as stronger base and hence it accepts proton from an acid. So, water causes interference in the reactions of weak base with an acid. In the same way, when a weakly acidic drug is present, then water with H^+ ion behaves like a strong acid and hence donates proton to the base. So, water causes interference in the reaction of weak acid with a base.

So, it can be concluded that in the presence of water, titration of either weakly acidic substances with stronger base or weakly basic substances with stronger acid is not possible. So, non-aqueous titration method is adopted.

Temperature Effects in Non-aqueous Titration

Non-aqueous solvents have greater co-efficients of expansion than water. So, small temperature differences can result in significant errors unless suitable correction factors are used. So, standardization and titration must be done at the same temperature. If it is not done in same temperature then the volume of titrant is to be corrected by the following formula:

$$V_c = V[1 + 0.0011(t_1 - t_2)]$$

Here, V_c = Corrected volume of titrant

V = Volume of titrant measured

t_1 = Temperature at which titrant was standardized

t_2 = Temperature at which titration was carried out.

Preparation of 0.1 N Perchloric Acid

(i) 8.5 ml of Perchloric acid (72%) is mixed with 500 ml of glacial acetic acid and 21 ml of acetic anhydride. This is cooled and glacial acetic acid is added to make 1000 ml.

(ii) 11 ml of Perchloric acid (60%) is mixed with 500 ml of glacial acetic acid and 30 ml of acetic anhydride. This is cooled and then glacial acetic acid is added to make the volume upto 1000 ml.

Then water determination is carried out. Water content is adjusted between 0.02% and 0.05% using acetic anhydride. Here the added acetic anhydride reacts with water to form acetic acid. Slight excess of acetic anhydride must be present but a large excess must be avoided. If large excess of acetic anhydride is present, they cause acetylation of primary and secondary amines to give non-basic products.

During preparation of normal solution of perchloric acid, firstly the perchloric acid is diluted with acetic acid and then acetic anhydride must be added. Otherwise, acetylperchlorate forms which is explosive in nature.

Standardisation of 0.1 N Perchloric Acid

0.7 g of potassium hydrogen phthalate is previously powered lightly and is dried for 2 hours. This is dissolved in 50 ml of glacial acetic acid. To this few drops of crystal violet solution is added as an indicator and is titrated with perchloric acid solution until emerald green colour develops from the violet colour. Then blank titration is done using 50 ml of glacial acetic acid. This is subtracted from the volume of perchloric acid consumed.

Each ml of 0.1 N perchloric acid is equivalent to 0.02042 g of K hydrogen phthalate.

Strength of 0.1 N perchloric acid

$$= \frac{\text{Wt. of KH phthalate taken}}{\text{Vol. of perchloric acid} \times 0.02042}$$

$$204.2 \text{ g of } C_8H_5O_4K \equiv 1 \text{ N } 1000 \text{ ml } HClO_4$$

$$0.02042 \text{ g of } C_8H_5O_4K \equiv 1 \text{ ml of } 0.1 \text{ N } HClO_4$$

$$C_6H_4(COOK)(COOH) + HClO_4 \longrightarrow C_6H_4(COOH)(COOH) + KClO_4$$

Preparation of Crystal Violet Solution (0.5% w/w in acetic acid)

Methods to determine end-point in NAT:

1. Potentiometric method
2. Indicator method

Most of the indicators are available to detect the end-point. They are prepared in AcOH. Sometimes methanol or dioxan is used.

Indicator	Colour Change		
	Basic	**Neutral**	**Acidic**
1. Crystal violet (0.5% in gl. AcOH)	Violet	Blue-green	Yellowish green
2. Quinaldine red (0.1% in MeOH)	Magenta	–	Almost colourless
3. Oracet blue B (0.5% in gl. AcOH)	Blue	Purple	Pink
4. α-naphthol benzene (0.2% in gl. AcOH)	Blue or Blue-green	Orange	Dark green

Applications of NAT (Non Aqueous Titration) to weak bases:

Application involves the following areas:

(1) Direct titration with 1°, 2° and 3° amines

(2) Titration of halogen acid salts of weak bases.

Direct titration with 1°, 2° and 3° amines: Here weighed quantity of sample is dissolved in glacial acetic acid and acetic anhydride. Then indicator is added to this solution. The contents of the flask are titrated against 0.1 N perchloric acid. 0.1 N perchloric acid is standardized by the above procedure which is written. Indicators used are crystal violet, α-naphthol, quinaldine red and oracet blue – B.

Potentiometric method can also be used to detect the end-point.

Raw materials or active ingredients (i.e., the drug without any other material like diluents) can be analysed by the above procedure. For drug formulations like tablets, the substance is needed to be extracted. Extraction is done with suitable organic solvents like chloroform. Then it is dissolved in glacial acetic acid. The contents of conical flask are titrated against 0.1 N perchloric acid using suitable indicator.

Examples of titration of amines and amine salts of organic salts:

Adrenaline, Codeine, Diazepam, Chlordiazepoxide, Ethionamide, Pyrimethamine and Metronidazole. Other organic base salts with organic acids inducle adrenaline acid tartar, chlorhexidine acetate, Bisacodyl suppositories, nitrazepam tablets, ethionamide tablets, salbutamol sulphate tablets, quinine sulphate tablets are the solid dose preparations analysed by this method. Amino acids like glycine, aminocaproic acid are also assayed.

Example 1: To determine the percentage purity of Nitrazepam:

Molecular formula: $C_{15}H_{11}N_3O_3$

Structure:

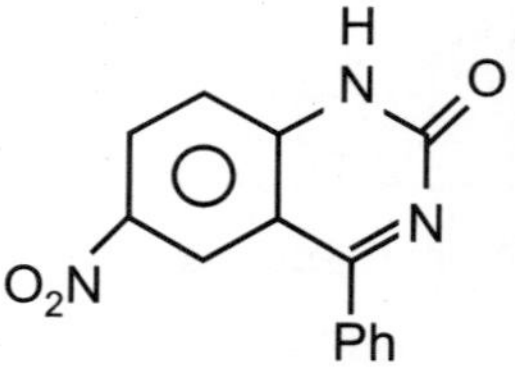

Procedure: 0.5 g of Nitrazepam is added to 50 ml of acetic anhydride. This is titrated with 0.1 M Perchloric acid using Nile blue A as indicator.

$$C_{15}H_{11}N_3O_3 \equiv HClO_4 \equiv 1000 \text{ ml M}$$

$$281.3 \text{ g } C_{15}H_{11}N_3O_3 = 1000 \text{ ml N}$$

$$0.0281 \text{ g } C_{15}H_{11}N_3O_3 = 1 \text{ ml } 0.1 \text{ M}$$

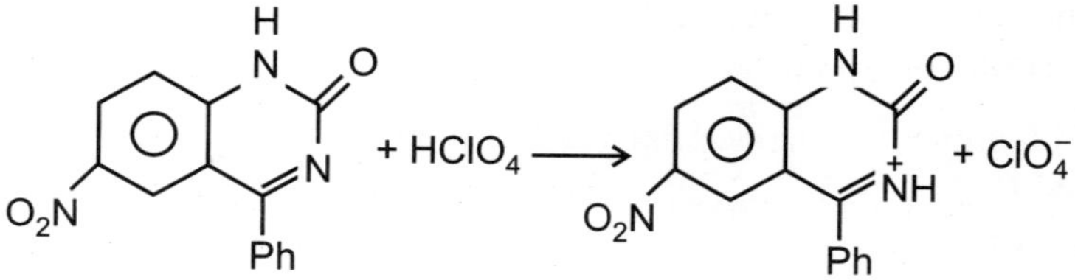

+ $HClO_4$ ⟶ + ClO_4^-

Titration of halogen acid salts of bases is assayed by the process of non-aqueous titration. The principle is based on the following facts:

Halide ions like chloride, bromide and iodide are too weakly basic in nature. They cannot react quantitatively with acetous perchloric acid. So, mercuric acetate is added. It is undissociated in acetic solution. Therefore addition of mercuric acetate to a halide salt replaces the halide ion by an equivalent quantity of acetate ion which is a strong base in acetic acid.

The reaction can be summarized as:

$$2R.NH_2.HCl \rightleftharpoons 2RNH_3^+ + 2Cl^-$$

$$\underset{\text{(Undissociated)}}{(CH_3COO)_2Hg} + 2Cl^- \longrightarrow \underset{\text{(Undissociated)}}{HgCl_2}$$

$$2CH_3COOCH_2^+ + 2CH_3COO^- \rightleftharpoons 4CH_3COOH$$

Amitriptyline HCl, chlorpromazine HCl, chlordiazepoxide, propanolol HCl, ephedrine HCl, Hyoscine HCl are analysed by this method.

Assay of chlorpromazine HCl:

Mol. formula $C_{17}H_{19}ClN_2S.HCl$

0.4 g of sample is dissolved in acetone.

Then mercuric acetate (10 ml; 5% w/v in gl. AcOH) is added and 0.2 ml of crystal violet (prepared as 0.5% in AcOH) solution is added. This is titrated with 0.1 M perchloric acid.

$$355.3\text{ g } C_{17}H_{19}ClN_2S.HCl \equiv 1000\text{ ml M } HClO_4$$

$$0.03553\text{ g } C_{17}H_{19}ClN_2S.HCl = 1\text{ ml } 0.1\text{ M } HClO_4$$

Non-aqueous titration of weakly acidic substances:

Many drugs are weakly acidic in nature. Such drugs are titrated with strong bases like potassium methoxide, sodium methoxide, Li methoxide, tetrabutyl ammonium hydroxide in toluene-MeOH solvent.

Application of titration with tetrabutyl ammonium hydroxide in the assay of drug include:

1. Assay of Ethosuximide (cyclic imide)

2. Assay of Bendrofluazide, Hydrochlorthiazide (thiazides)
3. Assay of Danthron, Oxyclozanide, Dichlorophen (phenols)
4. Assay of sulphafurazole (sulphonamides)

Preparation of 0.1 M tetrabutylammonium hydroxide in toluene methanol:

Dissolve 40 g of tetrabutyl ammonium iodide in 90 ml of absolute MeOH. To this add finely powdered purified silver oxide (20 g). This is to be shaken for 1 hour. Centrifuge a few ml of this mixture. Test the supernatant liquid for iodide. If reaction is positive then add an additional 2 g of silver oxide and shake for further 30 minutes continually. This procedure is to be repeated until the liquid is free from iodide. Then the mixture is to be filtered via a fine sintered glass filter. Reaction vessel is to be rinsed with 3 portions of 50 ml of dry toluene. Add these washings to the filtrate and dilute with dry toluene. This solution is flushed with CO_2 free N_2 for 5 minutes. Storage needs protection from CO_2 and moisture.

Standarisation of 0.1 M tetra butyl ammonium hydroxide:

Procedure: About 60 mg of benzoic acid is weighed. To this 10 ml of DMF is added. This DMF is previously neutralized to the full blue colour of thymol blue (3 drops; 0.3% w/v in MeOH) by titration with 0.1 M tetra butyl ammonium hydroxide. Benzoic acid is allowed to dissolved. This is then titrated in an atm. of CO_2 free N_2 with 0.1 M tetra butyl ammonium hydroxide.

Example 2: To determine the percentage of Ethosuximide

This titration is carried out in DMF using magneson solution as indicator.

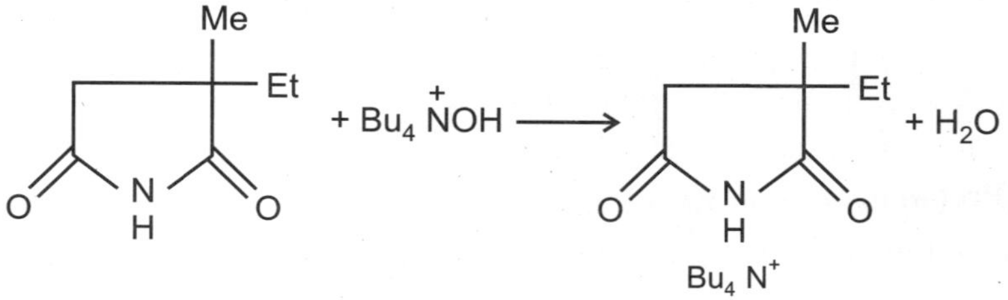

$\therefore \quad C_7H_{11}NO_2 \equiv Bu_4N^+OH \equiv 1000 \text{ ml M}$

$\therefore \quad 141.2 \text{ g } C_7H_{11}NO_2 = 1000 \text{ ml M}$

$\therefore \quad 0.01412 \text{ g } C_7H_{11}NO_2 = 1 \text{ ml } 0.1 \text{ M}$

Other examples:

(i) Fluorouracil (ii) Mercaptopurine.

Assay of Chlorthalidone

Procedure: 0.3 g of sample is dissolved in 50 ml of dehydrated pyridine. This is then titrated with 0.1 N tetrabutyl ammonium hydroxide. End-point is determined potentiometrically. The solution and the titrant must be protected from atm. CO_2 throughout the determination. A blank determination can be performed to make suitable correction.

Each ml of 0.1 N tetra butyl ammonium hydroxide is equivalent to 0.03388 g of $C_{14}H_{11}ClN_2O_4S$.

Equation may be represented as:

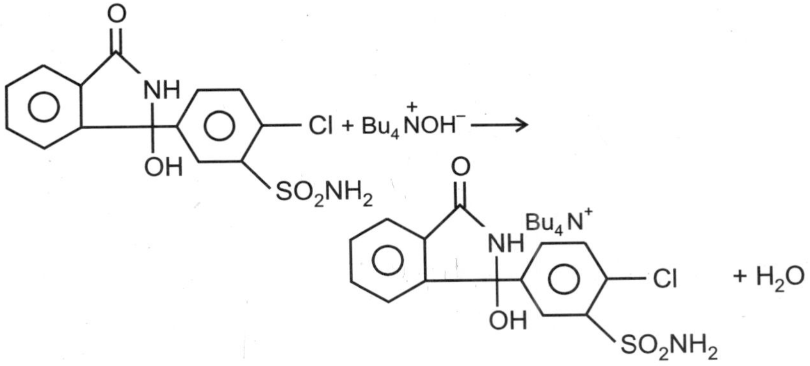

O NH OH Cl + $Bu_4\overset{+}{N}OH^-$ ⟶ SO_2NH_2

O NH Bu_4N^+ Cl + H_2O OH SO_2NH_2

Calculations:

$C_{14}H_{11}ClN_2O_4S \cong Bu_4N^+OH^- \cong H \cong 1000 \text{ ml N}$

$338.76 \text{ g } C_{14}H_{11}ClN_2O_4S \cong 1000 \text{ ml N}$

$0.0338 \text{ g } C_{14}H_{11}ClN_2O_4S \cong 1 \text{ ml } 0.1 \text{ N}$

Preparation and standardization of 0.1 N sodium methoxide:

150 ml of MeOH is taken in a volumetric flask and is cooled in ice. To this 2.5 g of freshly cut Na metal is added.

When metal gets dissolved then enough benzene is added to make 1000 ml and mix. This is stored in the reservoir of an automatic delivery burette to protect from CO_2 and H_2O.

0.4 g of benzoic acid is weighed (this is a primary standard) in a flask. This is dissolved in 80 ml of DMF and titrated with sodium methoxide using thymol blue (1 in 100 ml DMF) as indicator. End-point is blue in colour.

Each 12.21 mg of PhCOOH is equivalent to 1 ml of 0.1 N $NaOCH_3$.

The RK involved with Na and MeOH is:

$$Na + CH_3OH \longrightarrow CH_3O^-N^+a + \frac{1}{2} H_2$$

CO_2 and moisture must be kept away from sodium methoxide as following RKs may occur:

$$H_2O + CH_3O^-Na^+ \longrightarrow CH_3OH + NaOH$$

$$H_2CO_3 + 2CH_3O^-Na^+ \longrightarrow 2CH_3OH + Na_2CO_3$$

The other RKs involved are:

$$C_6H_5COOH + HCON(CH_3)_2 \rightleftharpoons HCONH^+ - (CH_3)_2 + C_6H_5COO^-$$

$$CH_3ONa \rightleftharpoons CH_3O^- + Na^+$$

$$HCON^-H^+(CH_3)_2 + CH_3O^- \rightleftharpoons HCON\ (CH_3)_2 + CH_3OH$$

$$C_6H_5COOH + CH_3O^-Na^+ \rightleftharpoons C_6H_5COO^-Na^+ + CH_3OH$$

Example 3: To determine the percent of purity of phenobarbitone

Procedure: Take 40 ml of DMF in a titration flask. To this add 3 drops of quinaldine red solution (0.1% w/v in EtOH) as indicator. This is neutralised by titrating with N/10 Li methoxide. Then 0.2 g of drug sample is taken in flask. This is titrated with 0.1 N Li methoxide using quinaldine red as indicator. Any contamination is needed to be avoided with H_2O and CO_2. End-point is detected when the colour changes from pink to colourless.

$$O=C\begin{matrix} \diagup NH-CO \diagdown \\ \diagdown NH-CO \diagup \end{matrix} C \begin{matrix} \diagup C_2H_5 \\ \diagdown C_6H_5 \end{matrix}$$

$$+ \text{LiOMe} \longrightarrow O=C\begin{matrix} \diagup NH-CO \diagdown \\ \diagdown \underset{\underset{Li}{|}}{N}-CO \diagup \end{matrix} C \begin{matrix} \diagup C_2H_5 \\ \diagdown C_6H_5 \end{matrix} + \text{MeOH}$$

❑❑❑❑

CHAPTER 5

PRECIPITATION TITRATION

Precipitation is the process of combination of two ionic species to form a very insoluble product. The reactions in titrimetric analysis occurs in a quantitative manner. It must proceed completely to form the product of the reaction. This type of reaction is neutralization, redox, complexation and of precipitation reactions.

The reactions in titrimetric analysis must include the following requirements:

1. The precipitate must be practically insoluble.
2. Precipitation reaction must occur in a quantitative manner.
3. The reaction should be rapid.
4. The titration results must be damaged due to absorption or any kind of co-precipitation effects.
5. Determination of equivalence point during the titration must be detectable.

PRINCIPLE OF PRECIPITATION

Solubility depends on the solvent and temperature. It is the concentrate of the dissolved solute in moles/litre when the solution is in equilibrium with a solid solute. In order to dissolve a solid, the intermolecular forces of attraction must be overcome, i.e., solute-solute attraction is replaced by solute-solvent attraction. Here the solvent competes with crystal forces and overcomes them. This means that the solvent environment must be similar to that provided by the crystal structure, i.e., "like dissolves like". But during precipitation, opposite thing happens. Here in precipitation intermolecular forces between the molecules of product are high. So solute-solute forces replace the solute-solvent forces.

Solubility Product and Precipitation

Here an aqueous solution of a slightly soluble salt BA is considered BA is in equilibrium with excess of the solid at constant temperature.

At equilibrium the reaction is represented as:

$$BA(s) \rightleftharpoons B^+ + A^- \qquad ...(i)$$

BA(s) is the solid phase. In dilute aqueous solution there is no undissociated BA present. The activity of solid is constant.

So, the equilibrium constant for (i) is:

$$K_{sp} = [B^+]\,[A^-]$$

K_{sp} is solubility product. This solubility product is a constant for a given solute, solvent and temperature condition.

Solubility product helps in calculation of one of the ion concentrate if the other is known. A substance precipitates if the product of the ionic concentrate exceeds at K_{sp} value.

This means that in equation (i) solid BA will precipitate out if the product $[B^+]$ and $[A^-]$ exceeds K_{sp}.

Example: Calculate the solubility product of $MgCO_3$ if 1 litre of its saturated solution contains 0.533 g of $MgCO_3$ at 20°C

$$MgCO_3 \rightleftharpoons Mg^{2+} + CO_3^{2-}$$

$$K_{sp}\ (MgCO_3) = [Mg]^{2+}\ [CO_3]^{2-}$$

Moleculer weight of $MgCO_3$ = 84.32

∴ The molar solubility of $MgCO_3$ will be

$$\frac{0.533}{84.32} = 0.00632$$

$$= 6.32 \times 10^{-3} \text{ mole/litre}$$

Since each mole of $MgCO_3$ on dissociation forms 1 gm ion Mg^{2+} and 1 gm ion of CO_3^{2-}.

∴ Mg^{2+} and CO_3^{2-} ions in the solution have the same concentrate equal to molar solubility.

$$[Mg]^{2+} = [CO_3^{2-}] = 6.32 \times 10^{-3}$$

$$K_{sp}\ (MgCO_3) = [Mg^{2+}]\ [CO_3^{2-}]$$

$$= 6.32 \times 10^{-3} \times 6.32 \times 10^{-3}$$

$$= 4 \times 10^{-6}$$

∴ The solubility product of $MgCO_3 = 4 \times 10^{-6}$.

Common Ion Effect

This effect provides a method for controlling the concentrate of the ions furnished by a weak electrolyte. That is, the solubility of any slightly solute salt can be decreased by adding an excess of either of its ions.

Example

The dissociation of a slightly soluble salt BA is:

$$BA(s) \rightleftharpoons B^+ + A^-$$

$$K_{sp} = [B^+]\ [A^-]$$

This is the equilibrium condition.

If in this case an excess of either B^+ or A^- are added whose solubility is greater than that of BA then the product of ionic concentrate $[B^+]$ $[A^-]$ will exceed the solubility product.

Therefore, [BA] will get precipitated.

Hence the common ion effect provides a valuable method for controlling the concentration of the ions furnished by a weak electrolyte.

In any solid system which is in equilibrium with its solution, the solubility product determines the product of the ion concentrations.

Example: If an excess of silver ion is added to saturated solution of AgCl in water then the solubility product of [Ag] [Cl] is exceeded.

Therefore, some Ag and Cl^- ions will be precipitated as AgCl. Equilibrium is reached when the product of Ag and Cl^- ions concentration becomes equally to the solubility product.

In volumetric analysis, quantitative precipitate can be utilized for estimations if the end-point at which precipitation is complete can be estimated.

Example: When $AgNO_3$ solution is added to a solution of NaCl, a ppt. of AgCl is formed, i.e., the reaction can be shown below:

$$NaCl + AgNO_3 \longrightarrow AgCl \downarrow + NaNO_3$$

Here the end-point is the point at which all of AgCl gets pted. But it becomes difficult to detect the end-point at which complete ppt. takes place. So, the end-point is generally detected by the formation of a coloured ppt. or a coloured solution at the end-point.

The following are the methods to determine the end-point:

(i) By potentiometry

(ii) By ampherometry

(iii) Appearance of turbidity or cessation of precipitation

(iv) Use of internal indicators.

In actual practice, this type of titration becomes more or less restricted since those involving ppt. of Ag^+ with anions is considered.

Example: Halogens like Cl^-, Br^-, I^- and thiocyanate SCN^-.

As already stated, in these precipitation reactions it becomes tedious to locate the exact point at which further addition of reagent causes no more ppt. (i.e., end-point of reaction). Here the choice of chemical reaction is made in a way so as to result in either a coloured solution or a coloured ppt. at the end-point.

Example: Use of potassium chromate solution (K_2CrO_4) in the above case cause any extra drop of $AgNO_3$, after all the Cl^- gets ppt. a change in colour. That is it causes immediate ppt. of red chromate which shows the end-point. This is also known as Argentometric titration. There are limitations to this type of ppt. titration.

(i) *Co-precipitation effect:* This effect does not give a real composition of the ppt.

(ii) Indicators are very limited.

The following four factors are to be considered for a feasible precipitation titration (argentometric titration):

(i) Insolubility of the precipitate. That is, the ppt. formed must be insoluble in nature.

(ii) The process of ppt. must be fast and rapid.

(iii) There must be minimal effects of co-precipitation.

(iv) Equivalence point or end-point of the reaction must be apparently visible.

Argentometric (or precipitation) titrations may be divided into two categories:

(i) Direct titration with silver nitrate.

(ii) Ammonium thiocyanate – Silver nitrate titrations (Volhard's method).

(iii) Pharmaceutical substances containing halides are estimated by direct titration with $AgNO_3$ solution as a titrant.

Preparation of 0.1 N Silver Nitrate Solution

16.989 g of silver nitrate is weighed and transferred into a volumetric flask. Then vol. is made with distilled water.

Standarisation of 0.1 N $AgNO_3$ solution

0.1 g of NaCl is weighed which was previously dried at 110°C for 2 hours. This is dissolved in 5 ml H_2O. To this 5 ml of acetic acid is added then 50 ml of MeOH and three drops of eosin solution. This is to be stirred on a magnetic stirrer. Then it is to be titrated with silver nitrate solution till the white particles of AgCl change to pink colour.

1 ml of 0.1 N silver nitrate is equivalent to 0.005844 g of sodium chloride.

Applications

(i) Determination of potassium chloride in pharmaceuticals.

(ii) Estimation of chloral hydrate.

(iii) Cognate assays.

The following pharmaceutical substances can be assayed by direct titration with silver nitrate using a suitable indicator.

(a) Benzyl trimethyl ammonium chloride (Dichlorofluoroscein is the indicator used)

(b) Iopanoic acid (Tetrabromophenolphthalein is the indicator used)

(c) Diatrizoate sodium (Tetrabromopethyl ester is the indicator used).

Mohr's Method

Determination of chloride ion conc. by titration method:

Introduction: Here the concentrate of chloride ion of a solution is determined by titration with $AgNO_3$ solution. Since silver nitrate is slowly added so a ppt. of AgCl forms.

$$Ag^+(aq) + Cl^-(aq) \longrightarrow AgCl(s)$$

When all chloride ions get ppt. then end-point of the titration results. Then additional chloride ions react with the chromate ions of the indicator solution, i.e., potassium chromatic. As a result of this reaction, a reddish brown ppt. of silver chromate is formed.

The reaction may be shown as:

$$2Ag^+(aq) + CrO_4^{2-}(aq) \longrightarrow Ag_2CrO_4(s)$$

Application of this Method

This method finds its use in determination of chloride ion conc. of water samples from many sources like sea water, stream water and river water.

Here the pH of the sample solutions should be between 6.5 and 10. But if the solutions are acidic then gravimetric method or Volhard's method of determination is to be applied.

Apparatus needed

1. Burette and Burette stand
2. Pipettes – 20 ml and 10 ml
3. Volumetric flask – 100 ml
4. Conical flasks – 250 ml
5. Measuring cylinders – 10 ml and 100 ml.

Solutions needed

1. Silver nitrate solution (0.1 ml/lit.):

5 g of silver nitrate is dried for 2 hours at 100°C. This is then cooled 4.25 g of solid $AgNO_3$ is dissolved in 250 ml of distilled water in a conical flask. This solution is then stored in brown bottle.

2. Preparation of potassium chromate indicator solution (0.25 mol/l solution):

This is prepared by dissolving 1 g of K_2CrO_4 dissolved in 20 ml of distilled water.

Procedure

Preparation of sample solution:

Sea water may contain traces of solid matter such as sand or seaweed. So sea water needs to be filtered before use. If not filtered then these solid matter will end up getting weighed along with AgCl ppt.

Titration Method

1. Sea water is diluted by pipetting a 20 ml sample into a 100 ml volumetric flask. Then it is marked with distilled water.
2. Then 10 ml of diluted sea water is taken in a conical flask. Then 50 ml of distilled water is added followed by 1 ml of chromate indicator.
3. This sample is titrated with 0.1 mol/lit. of silver nitrate solution. Firstly, silver chloride that forms is a white ppt.; the presence of chromate indicator initially gives the cloudy solution a faint

lemon-yellow colour. The end-point of the titration is identified as the first appearance of a red-brown colour of silver chromate.

4. This titration method is to be repeated with further aliquots of diluted sea water to get concordant results. Titre value must agree within 0.1 ml difference.
5. Titration must be stopped in the first trace of red-brown colour.

Calculations

1. Firstly determine the average volume of $AgNO_3$ used from the concordant titres.
2. Then moles silver nitrate reaction is to be calculated.
3. The following reaction is to be used to determine the moles of chloride ions reacting .

$$Ag^+(aq) + Cl^-(aq) \longrightarrow AgCl(s)$$

4. Then the concentrate of chloride ions in the diluted sea water is to be calculated.
5. Then the conc. of chloride ions in the original undiluted sea water is to be calculated.
6. Then the concentrate of NaCl in the sea water is to be calculated in mol/l, g/l and g/100 ml (%).

Points to Remember

1. Mohr titration must be carried out under conditions of 6.5 – 9 pH range. Since at higher pH, Ag ions get removed by ppt. with hydroxide ions and at low pH chromate ions get removed by an acid-base reaction to form hydrogen chromate ions or dichromate ions. So this affects the accuracy of end-point.
2. The method of Mohr titration is sensitive to the presence of both Cl^- and Br^- ions in solution. So this process will not be too accurate when there is some conc. of Br^- ion present in the solution in addition to chloride ion. In most cases, for example, sea water, the Br^- ion concentrate is negligible. Therefore, the

method can also be used to determine either the conc. of Cl^- and Br^- ions in total amount. Otherwise determination of Br^- can also be done provided Cl^- conc. is known to be negligible.

Volhard's Method

Volhard's method is Ammonium Thiocyanate – Silver nitrate titration process. This reaction is based on the following equation:

$$NH_4SCN + AgNO_3 \longrightarrow AgSCN \downarrow + NH_4NO_3$$

Here thiocyanate solution is always taken in the burette. This is added dropwise into the silver nitrate solution which is in conical flask. The silver nitrate solution must be acidified with nitric acid. FAS (ferric ammonium sulphate) is used as indicator. End point is the formation of a deep red colour of ferric thiocyanate. Ferric thiocyanate forms due to the interaction between Fe^{2+} ions with a trace of SCN^- ions. Nitric acid used in this method must be free from nitrous acid as the presence of nitrous acid will cause thiocyanic acid to give an instant red colour.

Titration is to be carried out at a temperature below 25°C since at elevated T the red colour of the ferric thiocyanate complex fades away rapidly Volhard's method needs complete ppt. of insoluble Ag^+ salts from HNO_3 solution by adding an excess of silver nitrate solution to the soluble salt. Then the excess of silver nitrate solution is estimated by residual titration with standardized ammonium thiocyanate solution. Here FAS is the indicator used.

Preparation of 0.1 N Ammonium Thiocyanate Solution

8 g Ammonium thiocyanate is weighed and volume is made upto 1000 ml in volume flask.

Standarisation of 0.1 N Ammonium Thiocyanate Solution

25 ml of 0.1 N silver nitrate solution is taken in an Iodine flask. This is to be diluted with 50 ml of distilled water. Then 2 ml of HNO_3 and 2 ml FAS are added. This mixture is titrated with ammonium thiocyanate solution to get the end-point. End-point is the appearance of red-brown colour.

Each ml of 0.1 N silver nitrate is equivalent to 0.007612 g of NH_4SCN.

Here after addition of ammonium thiocyanate, a white ppt. of silver thiocyanate is formed. Then a reddish-brown to colour appears. This colour fades out completely-shaking and therefore a white ppt. of silver thiocyanate forms. The appearance of a permanent faint reddish brown colour which does not vanish upon shaking is the indication of end-point.

Applications

1. Assay of Chlorobutol
2. Assay of Ethionamide
3. Assay of Aminophylline
4. Assay of NaCl
5. Mercury compounds like Phmercuric nitrate can be determined by titrating with ammonium thiocyanate solution. Then reaction is based on the following equation:

$$Hg(NO_3)_2 + 2NH_4SCN \longrightarrow Hg(SCN)_2 + 2NH_4NO_3$$

Adsorption Indicators

The use of adsorption indicators in precipitation titration is also known as Fajan's method. K. Fajan studied the nature of adsorption and introduced adsorption indicators in such titrations. Adsorption indicators are adsorbed on the surface of the ppt. at the equivalence point of titration. This adsorption results in change in colour.

Adsorption Indicators are Generally

(i) Acid dyes – *Example* : Fluorescein, eosin

(ii) Basic dyes – *Example* : Rhodamine series

Actually colloidal precipitate has the property to adsorb its own ions which are in excess. So this property is used in this method. For example, sodium chloride solution is titrated with $AgNO_3$ solution. Here NaCl ppt. adsorbs Cl^- ions which are initially in excess quantity. Therefore, the Cl^- ions form the primary adsorbed layer. This holds the secondary adsorbed layer of oppositely charged Na^+ ions. After equivalence point, Ag^+ ions are in excess quantity and therefore the Ag^+Cl^- ions adsorb Ag^+ ions as primary adsorbed layer. Then NO_3^- is the secondary adsorbed layer. In the presence of Na salt of fluorescein, the negatively charged fluorescein ion gets adsorbed instead of NO_3^- ion as secondary adsorbed layer. This process of adsorption occurs with a change to pink colour as a result of the formation of pink coloured complex of Ag^+ and also due to modified fluorescein ions. Another view suggests that during the adsorption of fluorescein ions a rearrangement of the structure of ion occur along with the formation of a coloured substance.

The following conditions are necessary for the choice of an adsorption indicator:

(i) The indicator ion must have opposite charge to that of the ion of the precipitating agent.

(ii) A colloidal state of the ppt. is desired. So, multivalent ions and other factors which have a coagulating effect must be avoided.

(iii) The solution should give sharp end-point. So it must be concentrated for the same.

(iv) Once the equivalence point is reached, the indicator should be secondarilly adsorbed.

Precipitation titration of halides (by argentometry) using adsorption indicators should be carried out with minimum light exposure because Ag halides are sensitive to the action of light by the layer of adsorbed dye stuff such as fluorescein.

Theory of Precipitation Titration

1. Titration curve for the titration of 50 ml of 0.1 M NaCl with 0.1 M $AgNO_3$.

(i) At the start of titration 0.01 ml $AgNO_3$ is added

$$[Cl^-] = 0.100 \text{ g ion/l} = 10^{-1} \text{ g ion/l}$$

$$-\log [Cl^-] = pCl = -\log 10^{-1} = -(-1) = 1.00$$

(ii) After adding 10 ml of $AgNO_3$ solution

Cl^- ion left in solution is 40 ml (as from 50 ml NaCl, 10 ml reacts with 10 ml $AgNO_3$).

$\therefore$ Total Vol. = 50 + 10 = 60 ml

$\therefore$ $[Cl^-]$ will be given by

$$40 \times 0.1 = 60 \times [Cl^-]$$

$$[Cl^-] = \frac{40 \times 0.1}{60} = 0.067 \text{ g ion/l}$$

$$pCl = -\log [Cl^-] = -\log [0.067] = 1.17$$

(iii) After adding 49.9 ml $AgNO_3$

Cl^- ion left is 0.1 ml is 0.1 M NaCl

$$\text{Total Vol.} = 50 + 49.9 = 99.9 \cong 100 \text{ ml}$$

$$0.1 \times 0.1 = 100 \times [Cl^-]$$

$$[Cl^-] = \frac{0.1 \times 0.1}{100} = 10^{-4} \text{ g ion/l}$$

$$pCl = -\log 10^{-4} = -(-4) = 4.00$$

(iv) After adding 50 ml $AgNO_3$ (equivalence point) neither Cl^- nor Ag^+ ions are in excess. Concentrate of these ions is given by square root of SAgCl (solubility product of AgCl).

$[Ag^+] \times | [Cl^-] = SAgCl = 1.0 \times 10^{-10}$

$$[Ag^+] = [Cl^-]$$

or

$$[Cl^-]^2 = 1.0 \times 10^{-10}$$

$$[Cl^-] = 1.0 \times 10^{-5}$$

$$pCl = -\log 10^{-5} = 5.00$$

(v) After adding 60 ml $AgNO_3$

Excess Ag^+ ions in solution = 10 ml 0.1 M

$$\text{Total Vol.} = 50 + 60 = 110 \text{ ml}$$

$$10 \times 0.1 = 110 \times [Ag^+]$$

$$[Ag^+] = \frac{10 \times 0.1}{110} = 9.1 \times 10^{-3} \text{ g ion/l}$$

Now $[Ag^+]\,[Cl^-] = 1.0 \times 10^{-10}$ (SAgCl)

$$[Ag^+]\,[Cl^-] = \frac{1.0 \times 10^{-10}}{9.1 \times 10^{-3}} = 1.1 \times 10^{-8}$$

$$pCl = \log (1.1 \times 10^{-8}) = 7.76$$

Calculation of Eq. wt. in precipitation titration

$$\text{Equivalent wt. of precipitant} = \frac{\text{Mol. wt.}}{\text{Valency of precipitating ions}}$$

Example: When KCl is added to $AgNO_3$, Ag^+ ion is ppted. as AgCl. Eq. wt. of $AgNO_3 = \frac{\text{Mol. wt.}}{\text{Valency of } Ag^+ \text{ ion}} = \frac{\text{M.wt.}}{1}$

2. Wt. of $BaCl_2$ = 0.5 g

50 ml 0.21 N $AgNO_3$ is added to ppt. AgCl.

Filter to remove ppt. excess of $AgNO_3$ is titrated with 0.28 N Pot. SCN to give 25.5 ml at end-point.

Find % $BaCl_2$ in sample

meq. of $AgNO_3$ added = 50 × 0.21 = 10.50

meq. of KSCN required = 25.5 × 0.28 = 7.14

Total meq. needed = 10.5 – 7.14 = 3.36 ml

$$\text{Amount of } BaCl_2 = \frac{3.36 \times 0.104 \times 100}{0.5} = 69.88\% \; BaCl_2$$

Fajan's Method

It was introduced in 1923-24 as a consequence to the study of nature of adsorption. Here adsorption indicators are used to detect the end-point. The principle is that at the end-point, the indicator gets adsorbed by the precipitate. During adsorption process, a change in colour of indicator takes place. This gives substance of different colour. So, they are the adsorption indicators.

The following indicators are used in titration of Cl^- against silver nitrate:

(i) **Fluorescein:** It is used for very dilute solution of Cl^- with silver nitrate. The solution must be neutral or faintly acidic. At end-point, there arises sudden change of white ppt. in greenish-yellow medium to distinctly red.

(ii) **Dichlorofluorescent:** It is used for very dilute solution of Cl^- (e.g., drinking water). The indicator works in the presence of acetic acid and weakly acid solution. End-point is from yellowish-green to red.

(iii) **Eosin:** Eosin is used for titration of Br^- and I^- with silver nitrate (from burette) in the presence of acetic acid. End-point is colour change from pink to reddish-violet. The halide ion is needed to be diluted to 100 ml.

(iv) **Di-iodo diethylfluroescein:** I^- are determined by this indicator. I^- must to diluted to 100 ml before adding this indicator. It works in neutral or weakly acid medium. End-point is change of colour from orange red to blue red. Here I^- is titrated with $AgNO_3$ (from burette).

Theory:

Theory is based on adsorption principle. When a solution of Cl^- ion is treated with a solution of $AgNO_3$, the precipitated NaCl adsorbs the excess of Cl^- ions. This is the primary adsorbed layer. The latter adsorbs secondary adsorbed layer of opposite charge present in solution. When end-point is reached, Ag^+ ions are present. They then get primary adsorbed and NO_3^- ions are held by secondary adsorption. For example, Na salt of fluorescein is used as an indicator, the negative fluorescein ion, is much more strongly adsorbed than NO_3^- ion get adsorbed on to the surface of precipitate. This adsorption does not retain the original colour of the indicator but forms a pink complex of Ag, also a modified fluoresceinate ion on the surface with the traces of Ag^+ ions.

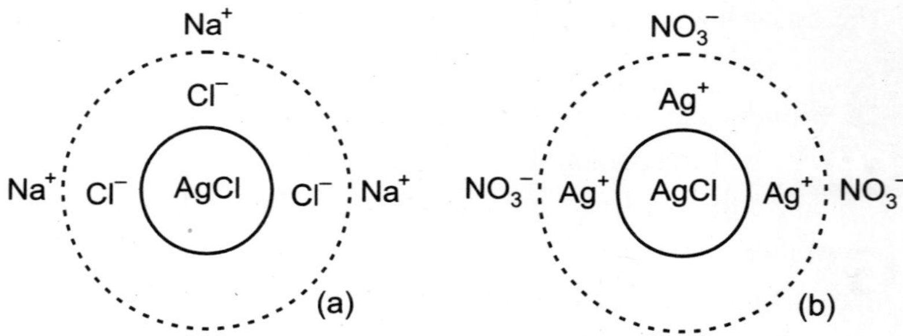

MERCUROMETRIC TITRATIONS

Principle

Here mercury ions are used as precipitants instead of silver. This process is an alternative method for the determination of Cl^-, Br^- thiocyanates and CN^-.

In this method, diphenyl carbazone or a mixture of diphenyl carbazone and bromophenol blue are used as indicator. At equivalence point, the yellow colour of the solutions turns blue-violet due to reaction of the excess of Hg ions with diphenyl carbazone so their absence is must. Other ions like Mg, Al, Mn, Zn, fluoride, SO_4^-, NO_3^- and acetate do not interfere at ↓ concentrate. The end-point in mercurometry is not very sharp in aqueous solution, so it is better to use 80% Ethanotic medium.

(i) **Preparation and standardization of 0.1 mercury nitrate solution:** 17 g of mercuric nitrate is dissolved in 800 ml of distilled water having 20 ml of 2 M nitric acid. This is diluted to 1 litre to get 0.1 N solution. Standardization is done as per silver nitrate ($AgNO_3$) solution using diphenyl carbazone or a mixture of diphenyl carbazone using bromophenol blue as indicator.

(ii) **Diphenyl carbazone mixed indicator:** The indicator is made by dissolving 100 mg of diphenyl carbazone in 100 ml of EtOH. 1 ml of this solution is used as indicator (i.e., diphenyl carbazone indicator). Mixed indicator is made by dissolving 0.5 g of diphenyl carbazone and 0.5 g of bromophenol blue in 100 ml of 95% ethanol.

❑❑❑❑

CHAPTER 6

GRAVIMETRIC ANALYSIS

Gravimetric Analysis is the technique by means of which an element or a compound is obtained in it's purest form via isolation techniques and subsequent weighings. The analysis involves the separation of element or compound from a specific portion of the pharmaceutical substance being determined. Then the weight of the constituent in the given sample is calculated on the basis of the weight of the product.

In gravimetric analysis, the final weight of the product is obtained by adopting any one of the below mentioned standard methods:

(i) Ignition or volatilization

(ii) Precipitation from solution

(iii) Solvent extraction.

Gravimetric analysis is based on the quantitative precipitation of the respective anion or cation from a given solution. The two methods are involved for this process. They are:

(i) as an insoluble compound with known composition.

(ii) as an insoluble compound which yields a residue.

The residue is having a specific composition after ignition.

The following steps are needed for a gravimetric analysis:

(i) Identification of an insoluble form with a definite composition.

(ii) Separation of the analyses properly from other constituents. If this step is not done then this may cause interference.

(iii) Washing of the ppt. in order to make it free from impurities and other coprecipitants.

THEORY OF GRAVIMETRIC ANALYSIS

The following theories account for gravimetric analysis:

(i) Law of mass action and reversible reactions.

(ii) Principles of solubility product.

(iii) Common ion effect.

Law of Reversible Reactions and Mass Action

Reversible Reactions

Reversible reactions are associated with quantitative analysis. These reactions under certain experimental parameters proceed to completion. In certain other conditions, they may even attain equilibrium before the reaction gets completed. So it is needed to establish the appropriate conditions whereby the reactions can move forward for attaining completion. This is the objective of quantitative analysis.

The following three parameters must be checked for the reversal processes. Because these parameters help in completion of the reaction:

(i) Formation of a sparingly soluble solid.

(ii) Formation of very slightly ionized molecules.

(iii) Formation of an insoluble gas.

Law of Mass Action

It states that the rate of a reaction is directly proportional to the product of molecular concentrates of the reacting substances.

Example: $BaCl_2 + H_2SO_4 \rightleftharpoons BaSO_4 + 2HCl$

Forward reaction

Rate of forward reaction is:

$$\text{Rate} = [BaCl_2] \times [H_2SO_4] \times K$$

$$K = \text{a constant}$$

Opposing reaction:

$$\text{Rate} = [BaSO_4] \times [HCl] \times K_1$$

$$K_1 = \text{another constant}$$

At equilibrium, rate of both forward and backward reactions are equal.

$$\therefore \quad [BaCl_2] \times [H_2SO_4] \times K = [BaSO_4] \times [HCl] \times K_1$$

$$\therefore \quad \frac{[BaCl_2][H_2SO_4]}{[BaSO_4][HCl]} = \frac{K}{K_1} = K$$

$$K = \text{Equilibrium constant.}$$

Principles of Solubility Product

The principle is stated in the following lines:

"The product of the concentration of the constituent ions in a saturated solution of a difficulty soluble salt for any given temperature is practically a constant. Each concentrate is raised to a power equal to the relative number of ions supplied by one molecule of the salt upon dissociation." This principle of solubility product finds its use in the following situations:

(i) Prevention of precipitation

(ii) Occurrence of precipitation

(iii) Difficult soluble salts in their saturated solution

(iv) Dissolution of a substance.

Let us consider a salt which gets solubilized in a difficult way.

Example: The salt A_pB_q on dissociation provides a relative number of p cations and q anions. This is expressed as:

$$A_pB_q \rightleftharpoons pA^+ + qB^-$$

∴ Solubility product of

$$A_pB_q = [A^+]^p \times [B^-]^q$$

[ ] is the expression of molar concentrates.

This matter is much cleared in the following example:

$$AgNO_3 + NaCl \longrightarrow AgCl \downarrow + NaNO_3$$

The above reaction shows that interaction of $AgNO_3$ and NaCl results in the formation of AgCl. The latter is slightly soluble in water. Experimentally it is found to be 1.5 mg/lit. or 0.00001 ml/lit. If this concentrate exceeds then there occurs precipitation of AgCl. This precipitated AgCl remains in equilibrium with the dissolved AgCl. So at equilibrium, the following reaction is seen:

$$\underset{\text{Solid ppt.}}{AgCl} \rightleftharpoons \underset{\text{Dissolved unionized}}{AgCl} \rightleftharpoons \underset{\text{Dissolved ionized}}{Ag^+ + Cl^-}$$

∴ The ionization equilibrium is written as:

$$\frac{[Ag^+][Cl^-]\text{ ionised}}{[AgCl]\text{ unionised}} = K$$

$$K = \text{Ionization constant}$$

Here it is assumed that the solution remains saturated with AgCl at a given temperature and also the concentrate of unionized AgCl remains constant.

∴ $K \times [AgCl]$ remains constant.

So it is stated that in a saturated solution of a difficultly solution salt, the product of the molecular concentrates of its ions is a constant.

The solubility product is expressed in terms of molar concentrations, i.e., moles/litre.

Common Ion Effect

There is no change in equilibrium constant even if the concentrate of reacting substances change and also even if the relative concentrate of reacting substances may change. For example: a solution of $BaCl_2$ is added to a solution of H_2SO_4, the SO_4^- ion present in a concentrate in a manner that causes its ionic product with the barium ion to exceed the solubility product of $BaSO_4$. Hence the insoluble $BaSO_4$ gets precipitated.

$$Ba^{2+} + SO_4^{2-} \longrightarrow BaSO_4\downarrow$$

At equilibrium the concentrate of Ba^{2+} ions = Concentrate of SO_4^- ions.

The supernatant liquid contains a saturated solution of $BaSO_4$.

The equilibrium which gives an idea of ionization constant is written as:

$$\frac{[Ba^{2+}][SO_4^{2-}]}{[BaSO_4]} = K$$

So it can be concluded that if the concentration of Ba^{2+} ion is ↑ by addition of soluble Ba salt, the concentration of SO_4^- ion ↓. Conversely if the concentrate of SO_4^- ion is ↑ by addition of a soluble SO_4^- salt then the concentrate of Ba^{2+} ion ↓ as their product remains constant. This ↓ in concentrate of ions in either case is achieved by combination of Ba^{2+} and SO_4^{2-} ions to form insoluble $BaSO_4$ which makes the RK to go towards completion. Hence the common ion effect is applied in gravimetric analysis of pharmaceutical substances to drive the reaction towards the product.

Gravimetric analysis helps in calculating the % of the desired constituent. The following equation is used:

$$\%\text{ of desired constituent} = \frac{\text{Wt. of ppt.} \times \text{Gravimetric factor}}{\text{Wt. of sample}} \times 100$$

Gravimetric factor = the number of gms. of the desired constituent in 1 g of the substance weighed.

Examples:

(i) 1 mole of silver chloride (143.322 g) contains 1 mole of Cl atoms (35.453 g)

$\therefore$ The gravimetric factor = $\frac{Cl}{AgCl} = \frac{35.453}{143.323} = 0.2474$

(ii) 1 mole of barium sulphate (233.39 g) contains 1 mole of SO_4 atoms (96.06 g)

$\therefore$ The gravimetric factor = $\frac{SO_4}{BaSO_4} = \frac{96.06}{233.39} = 0.4116$

A number of substances are estimated gravimetrically. The gravimetric methods adopted depend upon the nature of substances under determination.

The following types of substances are assayed by the process of gravimetry:

1. Those substances which can be assayed by gravimetric method.
2. Those substances which can be assayed only after conversion. They fall into the following categories:
   (i) Substances assayed after conversion to Free Acid
   (ii) Substances assayed after conversion to Free Base
   (iii) Substances assayed after conversion to Free Compound
   (iv) Substances assayed after conversion to Derivatives or Substitution products.

Substances Assayed Gravimetrically

Many pharmaceutical substances are analysed gravimetrically by their soluble salts as precipitates. The residue or precipitates are weighed to a constant weight. Then the percentage of purity of the substances is determined.

Example: Sodium chloride, Potassium alum.

Assay of Sodium Chloride by Gravimetric Method

0.2570 g of NaCl is weighed and dissolved in 100 ml of distilled water. To this 1 ml of dilute HNO_3 is added. It is stirred continuously. The resulting solution is checked for its acidity by blue litmus paper. 5 ml of $AgNO_3$ is pipetted to precipitate all the available chlorine as AgCl. The required amount of $AgNO_3$ must be added in small lots at a time. Constant stirring by glass rod is required. The beaker is to be covered with a watch glass. The contents is to be boiled gently. After this heating is to be stopped and the mixture is to be digested for 10 minutes in order to agglomerate the ppt. This enhances setting in order to have a clear supernatant liquid. 2 drops of $AgNO_3$ solution as to be added to the hot supernatant liquid to test whether the ppt. is completed. In other words, ppt. is to settled properly.

Then a Gooch crucible is taken and heated to a constant weight. This is fit into the suction flask. Then most of the supernatant liquid is to be decented into the Gooch crucible by gentle suction. The ppt. on the Gooch crucible is to be washed thrice with 15 ml portions of 0.01 N HNO_3. The filtrate must be free of $AgNO_3$. This is assured by testing. The ppt. is finally washed twice with 5 ml portion of distilled water in order to remove any trace of HNO_3. The trace of HNO_3 may get retained by the precipitate from the former wash solution. Then vigorous suction is to be applied to drain out the liquid from the ppt. to a maximum limit. Then this crucible is to be dried to a constant weight between 110-120°C in an electric oven to get two concurrent weightings. Then the weight of the crucible tare is to be deducted from the weight of the crucible plus the ppt. to arrive at the weight of AgCl.

Calculations

$$\underset{169.87}{AgNO_3} + \underset{58.44}{NaCl} \longrightarrow \underset{143.22}{AgCl} + \underset{84.99}{NaNO_3}$$

$$1 \text{ g of NaCl is equivalent to } \frac{169.87}{58.44} = 2.9067 \text{ g of } AgNO_3$$

Here 0.2570 g of NaCl is used.

$\therefore$ Exact amount of $AgNO_3$ required:

$$0.2570 \times 2.9067 = 0.7470 \text{ g of } AgNO_3$$

(Here NaCl is considered to be 100% pure)

Here 5% w/v of $AgNO_3$ is used.

1 ml of 5% $AgNO_3$ is equivalent to 0.05 g of $AgNO_3$

∴ The amount of $AgNO_3$ solution required = $\frac{0.7470}{0.05}$ = 14.94 ml

∴ The % purity of the given sample of NaCl:

$$\frac{58.44}{143.22} = 0.4078 \text{ of NaCl} = 1 \text{ g AgCl.}$$

The weight of AgCl is 0.6288 g (experimentally) or 0.4078 is the gravimetric factor.

$$\% \text{ purity of sample} = \frac{W \times E \times 100}{S}$$

Here W = Weight of the product of a chemical reaction with the substance under determination

E = Gravimetric factor

S = Weight of the sample.

Therefore, the % purity of NaCl in the given sample is:

$$\frac{0.6288 \times 0.4078 \times 100}{0.2570} = 99.77\%$$

Substances Assayed after Conversion to Free Acid

As already stated a few official compounds (substances) a assayed gravimetrically by using the steps such as separation purification and finally weighing the organic medicinal compound, without any permanent change in composition.

Usually, before extraction of an organic medicinal compound, the crushed tablets are washed with petroleum benzene to remove undesirable components like binders and lubricants which get exacted along with the organic medicinal compounds if solvents like ether or chloroform is employed. If the organic medicinal compound is acidic in nature like amobarbital in sodium amobarbital tablets then the following steps are needed:

The acidic organic medicinal compound is extracted with an aqueous solution of an acid or base to cause separation from the neutral substance which may be present. So the aqueous solution of the salt of the respective sample becomes acidic. Then the liberated organic acid (amobarbital) is extracted with ether or chloroform.

If Mg stearate or stearic acid is a component in the formulation, the acidic organic medicinal compound cannot be extracted with sodium hydroxide solution. It is due to the fact that sodium stearate also gets extracted along with the salt of organic acid. Hence, in the case, a saturated solution of $Ba(OH)_2$ is employed which results in the formation of insoluble ppt. of Ba stearate. The latter is discarded by filtration.

Example: Phenobarbitone sodium.

Procedure

0.5 g of phenobarbitone sodium is weighed. This is dissolved in 15 ml of distilled water. To this 5 ml of 2 M HCl is added. The resulting solution is extracted with 50 ml of ether. This is followed by successive 25 ml quantities of ether until extraction is complete. Then the combined extracts is to washed with 5 ml of distilled water two times. Then this aqueous extract is to be washed with 10 ml quantities of ether. This ether is to be added to the ethereal extract. Finally, evaporation is to be done in low bulk only. Then 2 ml of absolute EtOH is added. This is evaporated to dryness. As usual, the residue is dried to constant weight at 105°C.

Calculations

Each of residue is equivalent to $C_{12}H_{11}N_2NaO_3$.

$$C_{12}H_{11}N_2NaO_3 = C_{12}H_{11}N_2O_3$$

$$254.2 \text{ g } C_{12}H_{11}N_2NaO_3 = 232.2 \text{ g } C_{12}H_{12}N_2O_3$$

$$1.095 \text{ g } C_{12}H_{11}N_2NaO_3 = 1 \text{ g of } C_{12}H_{12}N_2O_3$$

Other examples include Phenyloin Sodium, Secobarbital Sodium.

Substances Assayed After Conversion to Free Base

If the organic medicinal compound is basic in nature then the following steps are taken:

(i) sample is treated with an aqueous solution of a base

(ii) then the liberated organic base is extracted with either $CHCl_3$ or ether.

Example: Papaverine in Papaverine HCl.

Method

Assay of Amodiaquine Hydrochloride

The principle is based on the ppt. of amodiaquine base which comes as a ppt. when the salt is decomposed in aqueous ammonia.

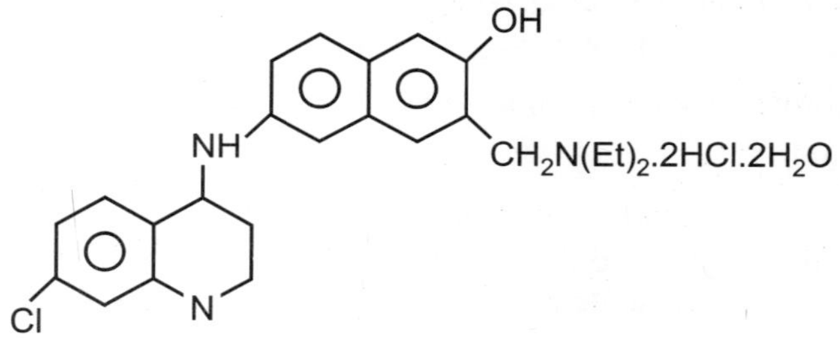

OH

NH

$CH_2N(Et)_2.2HCl.2H_2O$

Cl

N

$$C_{20}H_{22}ON_3Cl.2HCl.2H_2O + 2NH_3 \rightarrow \underset{\text{Amodiaquine base}}{C_{20}H_{22}ON_3 \downarrow} + 2NH_4Cl + 2H_2O$$

$$464.35 \text{ g of } C_{20}H_{22}ON_3Cl.2HCl.2H_2O \cong 355.4 \text{ g of } C_{20}H_{22}ON_3$$

$$1.306 \text{ g } C_{20}H_{22}ON_3Cl.2HCl.2H_2O \cong 1 \text{ g of } C_{20}H_{22}ON_3$$

Procedure

0.3 g of previously dried sample is taken in a 100 ml beaker having a stirring rod. It is to be covered with a watch glass. Then 50 ml of distilled water is added followed by dilute NH_3 solution. This is to be stirred properly until the solution becomes alkaline in nature (to litmus paper test). It is then kept for 30 minutes. After standing for 30 minutes, the solution is quantitatively filtered via No. 4 sintered glass crucible (previously dried to a constant weight at 105°C). The ppt. is then washed many times with distilled water. The residue is then dried to a constant weight at 105°C.

Each gm of residue is equivalent to 1.306 g of $C_{20}H_{22}ON_3Cl.2HCl.2H_2O$

Substance Assayed After Conversion to Free Compound

This method is used for certain medicinal agents like progesterone suspension sterile, progesterone tablets, sodium lauryl sulphate, mephobarbital tablets, sorbitan monooleate.

Experimental Procedure for Mephobarbital Tablets

20 tablets are weighed. After this, tablets are finely powdered and again weighed. Powder is equivalently weighed to 300 mg of Mephobarbital. This is extracted with 15 ml of hexane solvent. Extraction is done in an extraction thimble. After extracting with 15 ml of hexane solvent, the thimble is allowed to drain. Then it is transferred to a continuous extraction apparatus provided with a tared flask. Mephobarbital is extracted with chloroform for 2 hours. Chloroform is evaporated on a steam bath with the add of a current of air, then cooled and the residue is dissolved in 10 ml of alcohol. This is evaporated. Residue is dried at 105°C for 1 hour. It is cooled and weighed.

Result: The weight of the residue must represent the weight $C_{13}H_{14}N_2O_3$ in the portion of tablets taken for analysis.

Substances Assayed After Conversion to Derivatives or Substitution Products

This method is applied in certain cases by invariably converting the organic pharmaceutical substances quantitatively to their corresponding derivatives. Derivative or substitution product is made by interaction of the compound with certain functional entities like

$$—CHO,\ -\overset{\overset{\displaystyle O}{\|}}{C}-,\ NH_2,\ -\ COOH,\ -OH,\ etc.$$

In many cases it is easy to get uniform substitution products of pharmaceutical substances quantitatively. For example, phenolphthalein tablet gives tetraiodo derivative of phenolphthalein.

But the number of organic substances analysed by this method is limited. It is due to:

(i) formation of products of side reactions simultaneously.

(ii) reversible nature of reactions.

EXPERIMENTS

1. Analysis of Benzyl Penicillin (Benzyl PnNa or K salt)

Principle

Benzyl Pn (its Na or K salt) is assayed gravimetrically by quantitative conversion to 1-ethyl piperidinium benzyl penicillin derivative. Here precipitation is caused by 1-Et piperidine. This occurs when the respective Na or K salt of Benzyl Penicillin gets converted with phosphoric acid to the penicillinic acid (which is the parent acid). Then extraction is done with amylalcohol.

The reactions are:

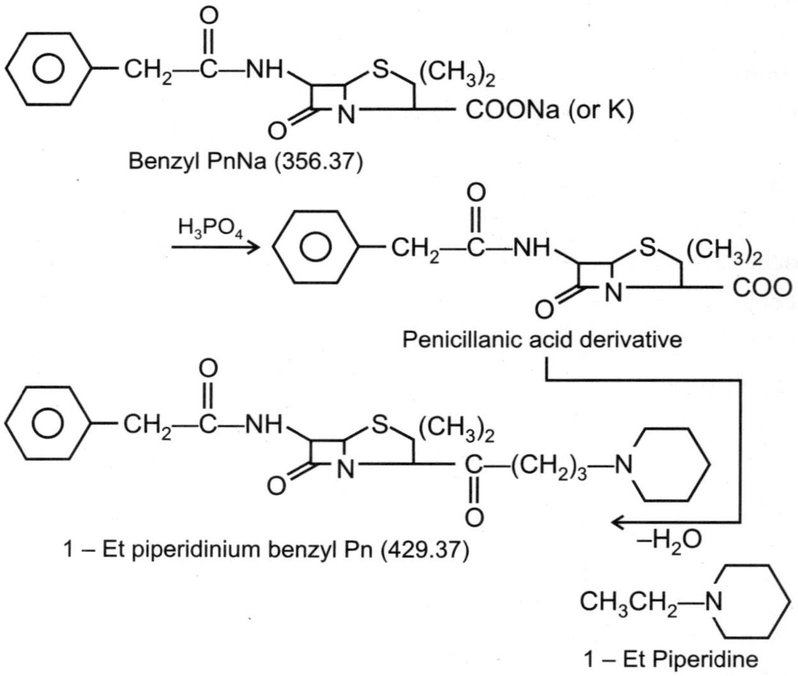

Benzyl PnNa (356.37)

$\xrightarrow{H_3PO_4}$

Penicillanic acid derivative

1 – Et piperidinium benzyl Pn (429.37)

$-H_2O$

CH_3CH_2—N

1 – Et Piperidine

Calculations:

$$C_{16}H_{17}N_2NaO_4S \equiv C_{23}H_{31}N_3O_3S$$

$$356.37 \text{ g } C_{16}H_{17}N_2NaO_4S \equiv 429.37 \text{ g } C_{23}H_{31}N_3O_3S$$

$$0.8300 \text{ g } C_{16}H_{17}N_2NaO_4S \equiv 1 \text{ g of } C_{23}H_{31}N_3O_3S$$

Procedure

0.12 g of sample (i.e., benzyl Pn Na) is to be weighed. Then it is dissolved in 5 ml of ice-cold distilled water in a flask. Cooling in an ice-bath is to be done. Then to it 5 ml of amyl acetate is added. After this 0.5 ml of ice-cold H_3PO_4 is to be added. This is stoppered. Contents is to be shaken for 15 seconds followed by centrifugation for 30 seconds. Then aqueous layer is to be removed by pipette. To this 0.5 g of anhydrous Na_2SO_4 is added. Contents are to be stirred vigorously. Then it is cooled in an ice bath for 5 minutes. Centrifuge for 30 seconds and cool again for 5 minutes in an ice-bath. 3 ml of supernatant liquid is pipetted out into a tared centrifuge tube. To this 3 ml of ice cold acetone is added followed by the addition of 1.5 ml of 1-Et piperidine amyl acetate solution. This is stirred. Then tube is to be stoppered and cooled in an ice-bath for 2 hours. This is then centrifuged for 1 minute. After this, the surface is broken via a pointed glass rod so that all crystalline particles are covered by liquid. This is again centrifuged for 1 minute. Then the supernatant liquid is decanted, ppt. is washed with 2 ml of ice-cold dry acetone in amyl acetate (which must be in ratio of 1:1). This is again centrifuged for 1:5 minutes followed by the process of decantation each time. This is dried to constant weight under vacuum at room temperature.

Each gm of residue is equivalent to 0.8300 g of $C_{16}H_{17}N_2NaO_4S$.

THIAMINE HCL

Gravimetric analysis of this compound depends upon the ppt. of it as thiamine silicotungstate with silicotungstic acid in a slightly acidic medium. Here the precipitating reagent is a complex silicate SiO_2, 12 WO_2, nH_2O. Degree of hydration has a variable composition.

The ppt. of insoluble thiamine silicotingstate is expressed by the following reactions:

$$2C_{12}H_{17}ON_4SCl, HCl + [SiO_2.12WO_3] + 6H_2O \longrightarrow (C_{12}H_{17}ON_4SCl_2); [SiO_2(OH)_2. 12NO_3]. 4H_2O$$

$$\therefore\ 674.6\, C_{12}H_{17}ON_4SCl, HCl = 34.80 \text{ g of Thiamine silicotungstate}$$

0.1958 g $C_{12}H_{17}ON_4SCl$, HCl = 1 g of Thiamine silicotungstate

Structure of Thiamine Silicotungstate

$$\left[\text{(4-amino-2-methylpyrimidin-5-yl)}CH_2-\overset{+}{N}\text{(thiazolium, 4-}CH_3\text{, 5-}CH_2CH_2OH) \right] Cl^-, HCl$$

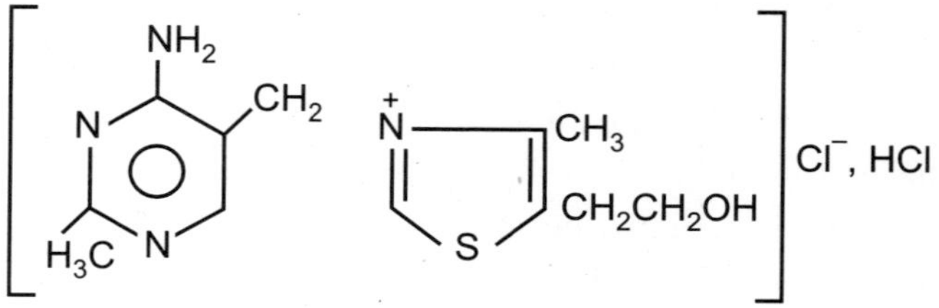

Procedure

0.05 g of thiamine HCl is weighed which is previously dried at 105°C. This is dissolved in 50 ml distilled water and stirred after a watch glass cover. To this 2 ml of HCl is added, and heated to boiling followed by 4 ml of silicotungstic acid solution. This solution is boiled for 2 minutes followed by filtration through a No. 4 sintered glass crucible which is previously dried at 105°C to a constant weight.

Then the residue is washed with a boiling mixture of HCl and H_2O (1:19). The mixture taken for washing is 40 ml. Then it is washed with 10 ml distilled water and two portions each of 5 ml acetone. Finally, the residue is dried at 105°C to constant weight.

Each g of thiamine silicotungstate residue is equivalent to 0.1938 g of $C_{12}H_{17}ON_4SCl$, HCl.

Examples of other compounds assayed by this method:

Histamine Acid Phosphate, Benzethonium chloride, Proguanil HCl, Pentolamine HCl, Piperazine citrate tablets, Iodochlorhydroxyquin Tablets.

Point to be remember

1. Coprecipitation

This is the unwanted material which precipitates along with the things not needed. Coprecipitation is seen to some degree in gravimetric analysis (e.g., $BaSO_4$ and those of hydrous oxides). One cannot avoid it but we can minimize coprecipitation by careful precipitation and proper washing.

2. In brief, Gravimetric Analysis is the measurement of mass. It is the quantitative method of determining the mass of a pure compound to which the analyte is related.

HISTORY OF GRAVIMETRIC ANALYSIS

Theodore W. Richards (1868-1928) and his students at Harvard developed this technique. They developed and refined many of the techniques of gravimetric analysis of silver and chloride. They developed these techniques to determine the atomic weights of 25 of the elements by following steps:

(i) firstly they prepared pure samples of the chlorides of the elements.

(ii) then decomposed known weights of the compounds.

(iii) after this they determined the chloride content by gravimetric methods.

This work made Richards the first American to receive the Nobel Prize in chemistry in the year of 1914.

Advantages of Gravimetric Analysis

(i) If methods are followed carefully, then it provides precise analysis.

(ii) Gravimetric Analysis was used to determine the atomic masses of many elements upto the accuracy of 6 figures.

(iii) There is no such instrumental error.

(iv) Due to high accuracy, if it is performed correctly then it an also be used to calibrate other instruments in lieu of reference standards.

Disadvantages of Gravimetric Analysis

(i) It usually provides for the analysis of a single element, or a limited group of elements at a time.

(ii) Methods often get convoluted. So if any mis-step occurs in the procedure then it can result in disaster of the analysis. For example, colloid formation in precipitation gravimetry.

Official drugs determined by Gravimetric Analysis – Barium Sulphate I.P.

CHAPTER 7

COMPLEXOMETRIC TITRATIONS

COMPLEXATION

It is the process of formation of complex chemical species by coordination of groups of atoms which are called as ligands to a central ion, which is a metal ion. Here, ligand coordinates by providing a pair of electrons that results in the formation of an ionic or covalent bond to the central ion.

Chelate

Chelate is a molecular structure where a heterocyclic ring is formed by the unshared electrons of neighbouring atoms. In other words, chelate is a coordination compound where a heterocyclic ring is formed by a metal bound to two atoms of the associated ligand.

Chelating Agent

A chelating agent is an organic compound where atoms form more than one coordinate bond with metals in solution. So, a chelating agent is a substance used in metal finishing to control or eliminate certain metallic ions present in undesirable quantities.

Chelation

Chelation is a chemical process which involves formation of a heterocyclic ring compound that contains at least one metal ion or H^+ ion in the ring.

THEORY OF COMPLEXOMETRIC ANALYSIS

Introduction

A complexing agent is an electron-donating ion or molecule, known as a ligand. This has its ability to form one or more covalent or dative bonds with the metal ion. It produces a complex. This complex has different properties from those of the free metal ion. So the metal will not get precipitated from the complex by the metal ion precipitants.

The stability of complexes varies to a large extent. The greater is the stability, the greater is the difference in properties from those of the original cations.

Many pharmaceutical inorganic substances contain polyvalent and bivalent metal ions. Previously Al^{3+}, Ca^{2+}, Mg^{2+}, Bi^{2+} and Zn^{2+} were analysed quantitatively by gravimetric analysis. But these gravimetric procedures were time consuming and tedious as it involved the following steps such as precipitation, filtration, washing, drying and finally ignition to a constant weight.

The introduction of an analytical reagent disodium ethylene diaminetetra acetate (EDTA) is the latest titrimetric method that is used exclusively for the estimation of metals using metal ion indicators.

$$(HOOC{-}CH_2)_2\ddot{N}{-}CH_2{-}CH_2{-}\ddot{N}(CH_2{-}COOH)_2$$

EDTA

Bonding in Complexes

Bonds involved are either ordinary covalent bonds where both the metal and the ligand contributes one electron each. Further, bond may be co-ordinate bond where both electrons are contributed by the ligand. For example, hexacyanoferrate ion consists of three ordinary covalent bonds and three co-ordinate bonds. In the complex, bonds are identical hybrid bonds which are directed towards the apices of a regular octahedron.

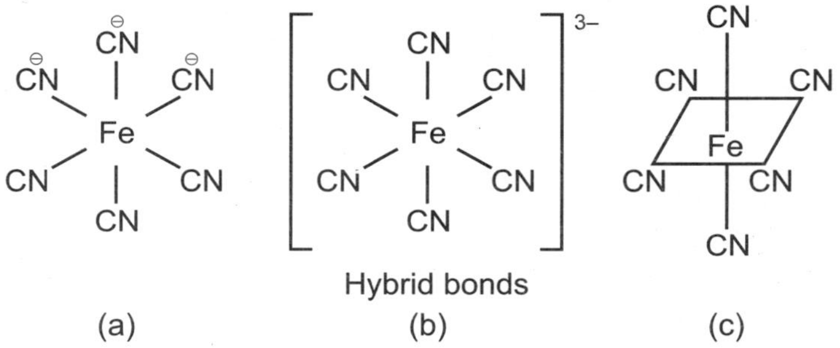

Hybrid bonds

(a) (b) (c)

Fig. 7.1: *The hexacyanoferrate iron (III) ion.*

Negative charge on complex = Total number of negative groups – the valency of the metal ion.

If neutral groups are only involved, then charge on the complex is positive and is equal to the valency of the metal ion, e.g., $[Cu(NH_3)_4]^{2+}$.

Werner's Co-ordination Number and Electronic Structure of Complex Ions

In 1891, Werner observed that for each atom there is an observed maximum number of small groups which can be accommodated around it. This number is called as Werner's co-ordination number which depends on steric factors and not to the valency of the ion.

The valency shell of the elements of the third period can expand upto 18 electrons and fourth one upto 32 electrons. So, a limit is there to the number of small groups that can be accommodated due to the limitations of space around the ion. For example, 4 is the maximum number for 2nd period and 6 is the maximum number for 3rd one. In case of molybdenum and tungsten it is 8.

Werner's co-ordination number suggests that there is a tendency for the metal to approach inert gas structure. This is the driving force for complex formation. Solubility of both chelating agent and metalchelate decreases in the absence of hydrophilic group. But they will be soluble in solvents which are organic in nature.

Sequestering Agent

They are the chelating agents which form water-soluble complexes with bi- or polyvalent metal ions. Even though the metals remain in solutions, they do not give normal ionic reactions, e.g., EDTA.

Dimethylglyoxime and salicylaloloxime are chelating agents which form insoluble complexes.

As a sequestering agent, EDTA reacts with many polyvalent metal ions to form water soluble complexes. In case of dimethylglyoxime and salicylaldoxime form complexes. Which are insoluble in water but are soluble in oraganic solvents.

Structures

$CH_3—C = NOH$
$|$
$CH_3—C = NOH$

Dimethylglyoxime

CH = N—OH
OH

Salicylaldoxime

Chelating Agents

Complexes with simple ligands, i.e., those having only one bond are co-ordination compounds ligands with more than one electron-donating group are chelating agents. The word chelating agent is derived from a Greek word which means claw. It is because they combine with metal ions in a manner which is like crabs claw to form cyclic structures, e.g., 1, 2-diaminoethane (ethylenediamine) act like two NH_3 molecules and form chelates with cobalt and copper ions.

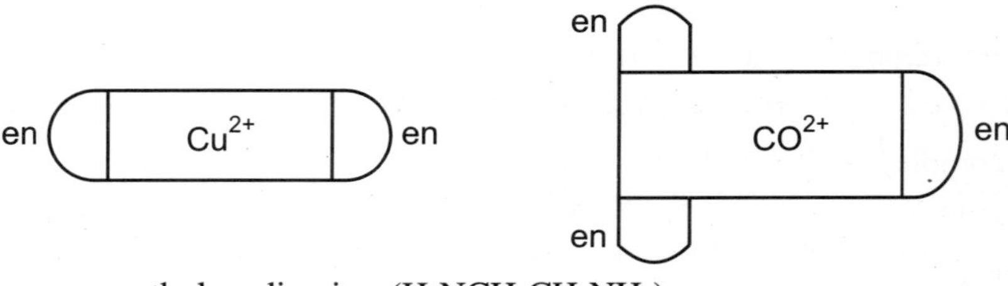

en = ethylenediamine ($H_2NCH_2CH_2NH_2$)

There is no much difference between chelate and co-ordination compounds. But in case of chelates, ring size influences stability.

It is observed in many organic compounds with chelate metals that if they contain groups with easily replaceable proton, e.g., —COOH group, OH group which may be phenolic or enolic) or neutral groups with lone pair of electrons (like NH_2, CO and alc. OH), then the structure of the molecules are such as to permit the formation of stable rings. The greater the number of rings formed the greater is the stability of the chelate. Rings formed in chelates need a higher or highest valency state of the metal. This is because they are more stable as compared to those having lower valency states.

If hydrophilic groups like COOH, SO_3H, NH_2 and OH are present then the solubility of metal of chelates in water increases. If both basic as well as acidic groups are present, then the complex becomes soluble over a wide range of pH.

Stability of Complexes

The equation for the formation of 1:1 chelate complex, MX is shown below:

$$M + X \rightleftharpoons MX$$

Here, M is metal ion

X is chelating ion.

The stability of the above reaction is shown by the equation:

$$\text{Stability constant (K)} = \frac{[MX]}{[M][X]}$$

Here [ ] shows activities.

Rise in temperature causes a slight increase in ionization of the complex and lowering of stability constant K. Electrolytes with no common ion with the complex decreases the value of K. But the presence of Ethanol increases K value due to the suppression of ionization.

Titration Curve

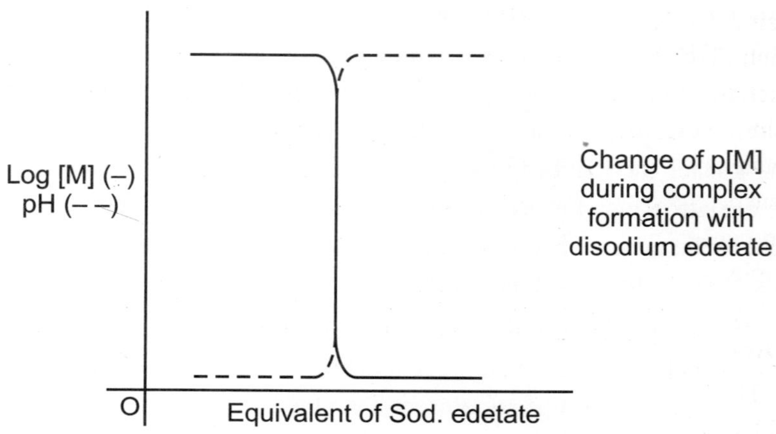

Titration of Metal Ions using Disodium Edentate

Edetic acid is only sparingly soluble in water, i.e., about 0.2%. But disodium salt has a solubility of about 10%. So disodium salt is generally used. When disodium edetate solution is added into a solution of a metal ion (previously buffered to promote efficient complex formation), then the rate of change of concentrate of metal ion is slow firstly but then it raises very rapidly. Rise occurs as the amount of disodium edetate added approaches one equivalent. This process can be compared with the change in H^+ concentrate (pH) during the titration of a strong acid with a strong base.

Types of Complexometric Titrations

1. Direct Titration:

As the name suggests, a suitable buffer solution and indicator are added to the metal ion solution. This solution is then titrated with standard disodium edetate until the indicator colour just changes. A blank titration is done to check the presence of traces of metallic impurities in the reagents.

2. Back Titration:

This method is used in case of metals which get precipitated as hydroxides from solution at the required pH for titration. Further, the method also finds use for insoluble substances like lead as sulphate, calcium as oxalate. Back titration method is also used for substances which do not react quickly with disodium edetate. Those metal ions which form more stable complexes with disodium edetate than with the desired indicator, this method is used. Here excess of standard sodium edetate and a suitable buffer solution is treated with the metal solution or suspension. This solution is heated to have complex formation. It is then cooled. Then the disodium edetate which is not required by the sample is then back titrated with Mg or Zinc chloride or Zinc sulphate. Suitable indicator is used.

3. Replacement of one complex by another:

This method is used when direct titration or back titration do not yield sharp end-points. In this process, metal can be determined by the displacement of an equivalent amount of Mg or Zn from a less stable edetate complex. This is shown by the following reaction:

$$M^{2+} + MgX^{2-} \longrightarrow MX^{2-} + Mg^{2+}$$

This method is used for the determination of Ca, Pb and Hg using Mordant Black II as an indicator.

4. Alkalimetric titration of metals:

Here, protons from disodium edetate are displaced by a heavy metal. This is titrated with standard alkali.

The equation is shown as:

$$M^{n+} + [H_2X]^{2-} \longrightarrow [MX]^{(n-4)} + 2H^+$$

This is alkalimetric titration is carried out in unbuffered solution. A visual pH indicator is used. But in cases when the colour of the complex would mask that of a pH indicator then potentiometric method of detection of end-point is suitable.

Complexometric Methods

Standardization of 0.05 M disodium edetate:

The method is based on the titration of disodium edetate solution with a standard Zinc chloride solution. The latter is prepared from a known weight of granulated zinc.

$$Zn + 2HCl \longrightarrow ZnCl_2 + H_2$$

Procedure

0.125 g of granulated zinc is weighed. It is dissolved in HCl (7 M). To this Br water is added (0.2 ml) so that oxidation of trace iron impurity to Fe(III) takes place. This forms a much less stable edetate complex than Fe(II). It is boiled gently to remove excess of bromine. This is cooled. Then add NaOH (2 M) until solution gets neutrality. This is diluted to 250 ml followed by addition of NH_3 buffer solution of pH 10 until the ppt. gets dissolved. Then this is added a little quantity in excess. Mordant black II and sodium chloride (1:99, 50 mg) mixture is added as an indicator. This solution is titrated with 0.05 M disodium edetate solution until the solution becomes green in colour.

Preparation of Ammonia buffer solution of pH 10

Dissolve 5.4 g of NH_4Cl in 5 M NH_3 (70 ml). This is diluted with water to 100 ml.

The reaction is:

$$ZnCl_2 + C_{10}H_{14}N_2NaO_8 \longrightarrow C_{10}H_{14}N_2O_8Zn + 2NaCl$$

$\therefore$ 65.38 g Zn $\equiv$ 1000 ml M

$\therefore$ 0.003269 g Zn $\equiv$ 1 ml 0.05 M disodium edetate.

Examples of substances assayed by direct titration with disodium EDTA:

1. Calcium Carbonate
2. Dibasic Ca Phosphate
3. Magnesium Chloride
4. Magnesium Trisilicate
5. Heavy Mg Oxide
6. Zinc Chloride
7. Zinc Stearate
8. Zinc Undecylenate
9. Zinc Sulphate.

Limitations of Direct Titration Method

In the assay of Al and Bi containing substances, direct titration method does not give proper result. It is due to the fact that the ppt. of the metal to its hydroxides occur in alkaline media. This gives erroneous results.

Example: Assay of Potassium alum, KAl $(SO_4)_2.12H_2O$.

Principle

Aluminium edetate complex is formed by heating the solution of potassium alum with an excess of disodium edetate. Hexamine acts as a buffer by stabilizing the pH between 5-6.

The reaction is:

$$Al^{3+} [H_2X]^{2-} \longrightarrow [AlX]^- + 2H^+$$

$$KAl(SO_4)_2.12H_2O \equiv Al_{3+} \equiv Na_2H_2X.\ 2H_2O$$

$$474.4\ g\ KAl(SO_4)_2.12H_2O \equiv 1000\ ml\ M$$

$$0.02372\ g\ KAl(SO_4)_2.12H_2O \equiv 1\ ml\ 0.05\ M\ disodium\ edetate.$$

This pH is ideal for the titration of the disodium edetate which is not used by Al. That is, the excess of disodium edetate is titrated with 0.05 M lead nitrate using Xylenol orange as indicator.

Procedure

0.6 g of sample is dissolved in 2 ml HCl and water (50 ml), then 50 ml of 0.05 M standard disodium edetate is added. This is neutralized with NaOH using Me red. It is boiled on water bath for 10 minutes and then cooled. 5 g of hexamine is added. A mixture of xylenol orange and potassium nitrate (1:99; 50 mg) is added as indicator. This solution is titrated with 0.05 M lead (II) nitrate. At end-point, the colour is changed from yellow to reddish purple.

Other examples:

1. Aluminium sulphate
2. Dried aluminium hydroxide.

End-Point Detection in Complexometric Titrations

The following are the physical methods employed:

Potentiometric Titration

Disodium edetate reacts with the higher valency state of an ion, so it can reduce the redox potential as per the equation:

$$E = E_o + \log_e \frac{[Ox.]}{[Red.]}$$

E = Potential of the electrode

E_o = Std. electrode potential

Ox. = Activity of ions in the oxidized state

Red. = Activity of ions in the reduced state.

Limitations:

1. Lack of suitable indicator electrode makes in method of limited value.
2. Amperometric titration.
3. Spectrophotometric detection.
4. High frequency titrator.

End-point detection in complexometric titration using pM indicators:

PM indicators help in detection of end-point. That is, the equivalence point in complexometric titrations is observed by the help of pM indicators. There exists a relation between pM, concentrates of ligand, chelate complex and stability constant. This is established by the following equations:

$$K = \frac{[MX]}{[M][X]}\text{; K = Stability constant}$$

$$[M] = \frac{[MX]}{[X]K}$$

$$\log [M] = \log \frac{[MX]}{[X]} - \log K$$

$$pM = \log \frac{[X]}{[MX]} - pK$$

If in the solution [X] = [MX], pM = –pK or pM = pK′, where K′ = dissociation constant.

In a solution having equal activities of metal complex and free chelating agent, the concentrate of metal ions remain roughly constant. It will be buffered in the same way as are H^+ ions in a pH buffer.

Chelating agents are also bases, so eq lb, in a metal-buffer solution is affected by a change in pH. For example, in case of chelating agents of the aminoacid type, like edetic acid and ammonia triacetic acid then [x] = [MX]. Here pM rises with pH till 10 then it attains a constant value. So, this pH is chosen for carrying out titration of metals with chelating agents in buffered solution.

Description of pH indicators:

1. PM indicator is a dye. It is capable of acting as a chelating agent to give a dye-metal complex.
2. Dye-metal complex has a different colour from the dye itself. It has a lower stability constant than the chelate-metal complex.
3. So the colour of the solution remains that of the dye-complex until end-point is reached, i.e., when an equivalent amount of sodium edetate has been added.
4. So if there is a slight excess of edetate in the solution then the metal-dye complex decomposes to produce free dye. This causes a change in colour.

Points to Remember

Along with pH, the colours of dyes and of the metal complexes vary. This fact is to be considered along with complex stability. In other word, it is necessary to decide at which pH to carry out a titration.

Further, it is vital to use a buffer solution to maintain the required pH during titration.

PM Indicators

The following are the pM indicators:

1. Alizarin fluorine blue (Alizarin complexone)
2. Calcon (mordant black 17)
3. Calcon carboxylic acid
4. Catechol violet

5. Methylthymol blue
6. Diphenylcarbazone
7. Dithizone (1, 5 Diphenylthiocarbazone)
8. Murexide (ammonium purpurate)
9. Mordant black II (Erichrome Black T, Solochrome Black T)
10. Mordant blue 3 (Solochrome cyanide R)
11. Xylenol orange
12. Sodium Alizarine sulphonate
13. Tiron (disodium, 1,2-dihydroxyphenol-3, 5-disulphonate)

1. Alizarin Fluorine Blue

It is used in acid solution at pH 4.3. Alizarin fluorine blue is used for the titration of Lead, Zinc, Cobalt (II), Mercury (II) and Copper (II) Here the colour changes frum red to yellow.

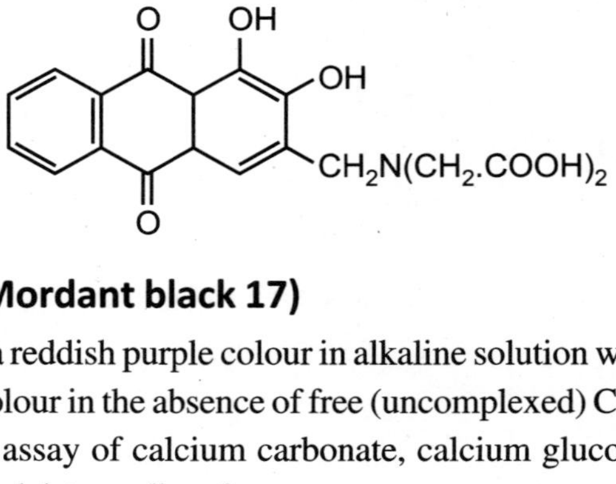

O OH OH $CH_2N(CH_2.COOH)_2$ O

2. Calcon (Mordant black 17)

Calcon gives a reddish purple colour in alkaline solution with calcium. It gives a blue colour in the absence of free (uncomplexed) Ca ions. Calcon is used in the assay of calcium carbonate, calcium gluconate, calcium chloride and calcium sodium lactate.

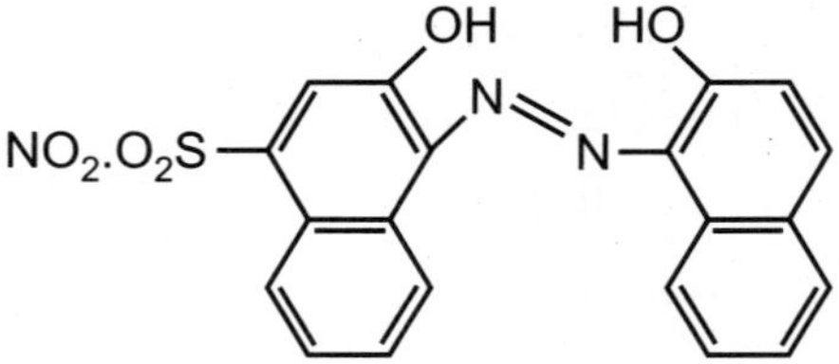

OH HO $NO_2.O_2S$ N N

Diphenylcarbazone

It is an indicator for mercury determination in the assay of propylthiouracil. The end-point is noted with the formation of a violet-coloured complex with Hg(II) ions. This reaction occurs for Hg in 0.2 M nitric acid, but there must be absence of chromates and molybdates. Copper, Fe, Co and other ions give coloured complexes in neutral or slightly acid solution chlorides form $(HgCl_4)^{2-}$ ions so it reduces the sensitivity to mercury.

$$2C_6H_5N = N.CO.NH.NHC_6H_5 + Hg^{2+}$$

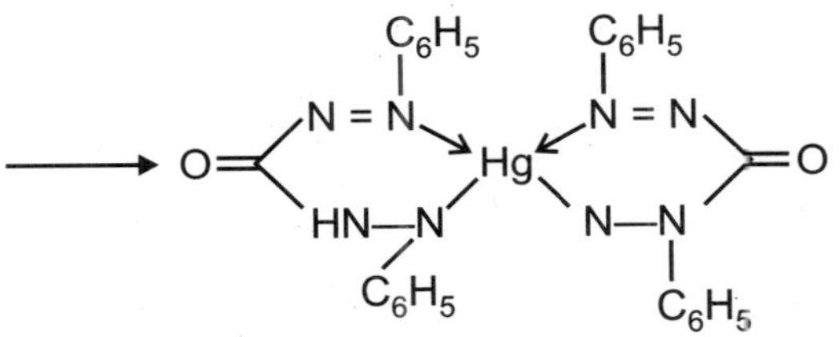

$\longrightarrow$

C_6H_5 C_6H_5
N = N N = N
O= Hg =O
HN—N N—N
C_6H_5 C_6H_5

Methyl Thymol Blue

Methyl thymol blue is derived from thymol blue.

It is used in following cases:

1. Used for Bi in strongly acid solution (M nitric acid).
2. Used for Pb, Zn, Cd, Hg(II) and Co(III) in weakly acid solution (hexamine buffer).
3. Pb, Zn, Cd, Co(II), Mg and Mn(II) can be determined using an $NH_4Cl^- NH_3$ buffer pH10 in alkaline solution.
4. In stronger alkali (0.05 M NaOH solution), Ca, Ba and strontium can be titrated.

A 1% aqueous solution of the dye is stable. Its colour changes from blue to grey in alkaline solution and blue to yellow in acid solution.

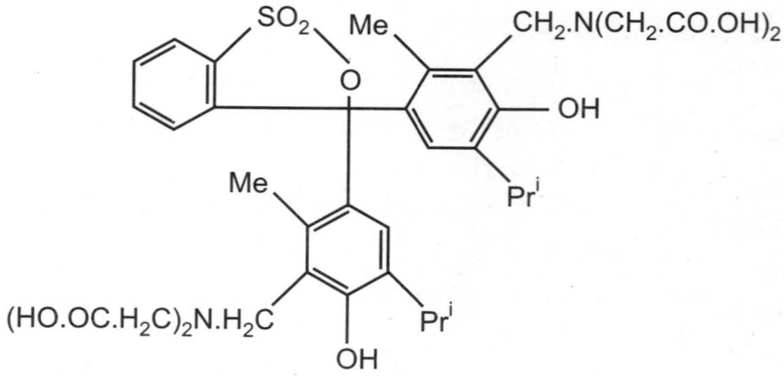

Mordant Black II (Erichrome Black T, Solochrome Black T)

This indicator is blue at pH 10. It forms reddish complexes mostly. The dye is reddish below pH 6.3 and above 11.5. So titration is carried out in the presence of buffer at pH 10.

Ca, Mg, Cd, Zn, Mn, Pb, Hg (II) and lanthanium are titrated directly by this indicator. But in case of Ba and strontium, back titration is to be done using std. $MgCl_2$ solution.

Mordant Blue 3 (Solochrome Cyanine R)

It gives a deep purple colour with Al ions in acidic solution. In the absence of free (uncomplexed) Al ions, it gives a pale pink colour.

Murexide (Ammonium Purpurate)

Ca is titrated using this at pH 12

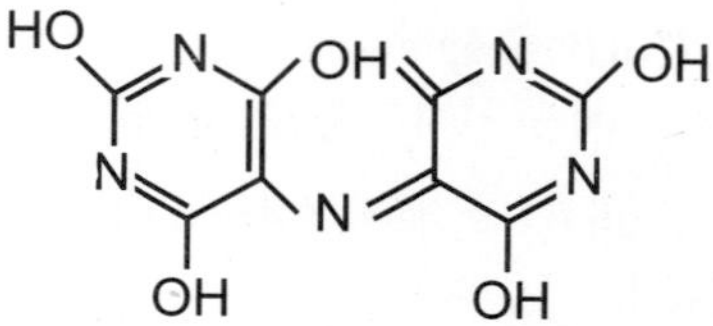

Mirexide (violet at pH12)

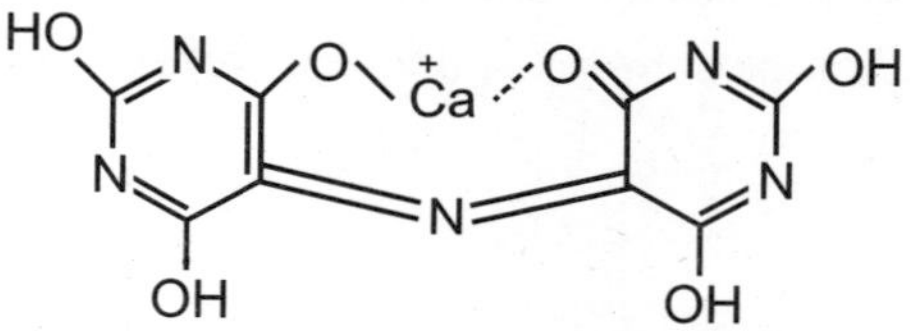

Ca–murexide

Cu, Co, Ni and Ce form yellow complexes with murexide in alkaline condition.

Xylenol Orange

Xylenol orange is an acid-base indicator. It has lemon-yellow colour in acid solution and red colour in alkaline solution. It gives red coloured metal complexes. So it is restricted to titrating metals which form stable edetate complexes in acid solution such as Bi, Pb, Cd and Hg. Stability of complexes varies with pH. Bi and thorium can be titrated from pH 1 to 3. Pb and Zn can be titrated from pH 4-5. Cd and Hg can be titrated from pH 5-6.

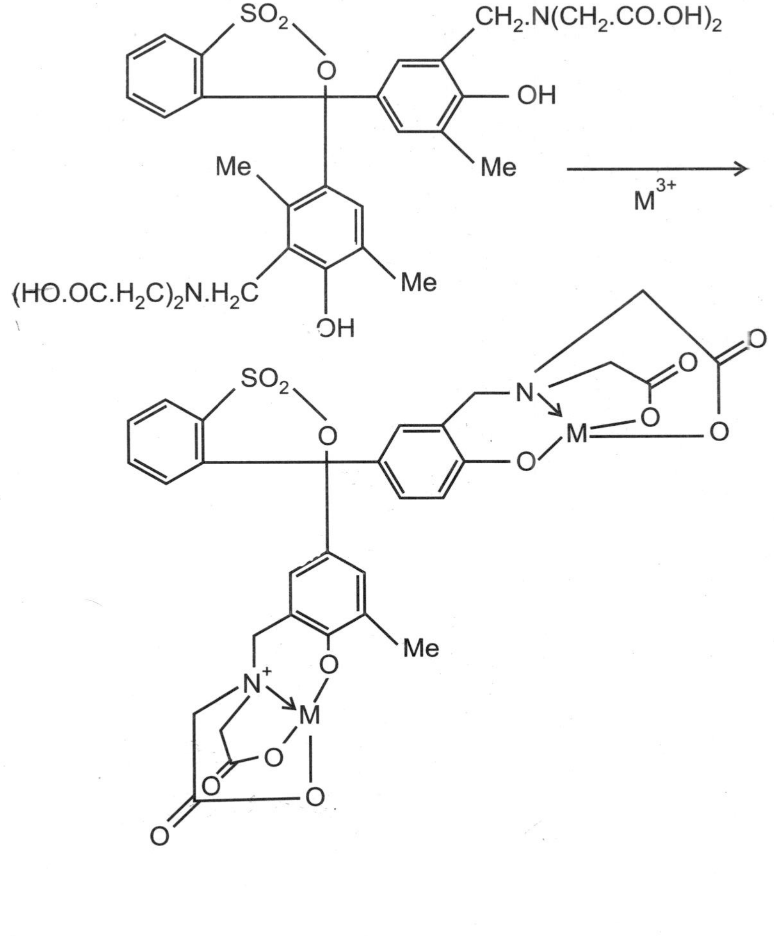

Masking and Demasking Agents

Since a wide range of cations get complexed with disodium edetate so method selection becomes improper. Metal impurities may get titrated along with the ion which is to be estimated. Thats why, masking agents are used in case where it is necessary to assay selectively one or more ions in a mixture of cations and also to eliminate the effects of possible impurities which would add to the titre.

Masking agents act either by ppt. or by formation of complexes which will be more stable than the interfering ion-edetate complex. It is vital that any colour due to ppt. or any auxiliary complexes should not interfere with the end-point.

Masking can be done by the following methods:

1. Masking by precipitation

When interference due to the following ions are encountered, the precipitants are added. The collected precipitates are then estimated separately.

Interfering ions	Precipitants
Cu, Co, Pb	Sodium sulphide, Thioacetamide
Pb, Ba	Sulphate
Pb, Ca	Oxalate
Pb, Ca, Mg	Fluoride
Zn, Cu	Ferrocyanide
Other heavy metals	8-Hydroxy quinoline, Cupferron

2. Addition of complexing agents

This results in formation of complexes with interfering ions. These complexes due more stable as compared to edetate complexes. So impurities are eliminated and selective titration can be done properly.

Interfering ions	Complexing agents
Al, Fe, Ti	Ammonium fluoride
Ferric	Ascorbic acid + Ferrocyanide

Hg, Cd, Zn, As, Sb	Dimercaprol in alkaline
Tin, Pb, Bi	Medium
Hg	KI

3. Control of pH

The edetate complexes with alkaline earth metals are it stable below pH 7. In this pH region and upto pH 3, complexes with Sn^{4+} (Tin), Fe^{3+}, Co^{3+} stable. So, they can be titrated selectively by varying pH.

Applications

Complexometric titration has application in the analysis of the following pharmaceuticals:

Al hydroxide gel	$MgCl_2$
Dried Al hydroxide gel	$MgSO_4$
Al_2SO_4	Dibasic $CaPo_4$
Al hydroxide tabs	Tribasic $CaPo_4$
$CaCO_3$	
$CaCl_2$	
Ca gluconate inj., tabs	
Ca lactate tabs	
$ZnCl_2$	
Zn stearate	
$ZnSO_4$	
TiO_2	

CHAPTER 8

DIAZOTISATION TITRATION

Aromatic primary amine moiety, i.e., Ar – NH_3 is present in sulphadrugs (like sulphamethoxazole, sulphaphenazole) and other potent pharmaceutical agents like Ca or Na aminosalicylate, dapsone, procaine HCl, primaquine phosphate and procainamide HCl. So, these drugs react with sodium nitrate in an acidic medium to yield diazonium salts.

The reaction is expressed as:

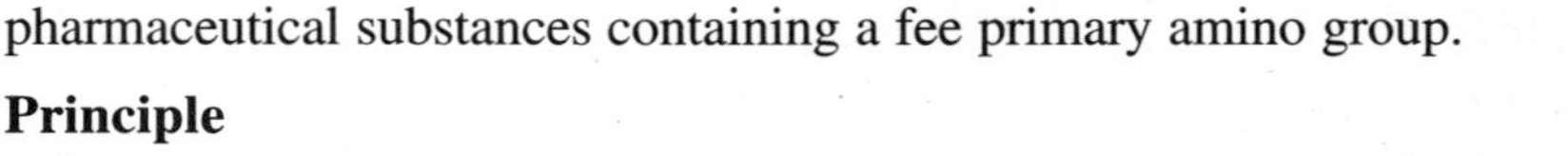

$$C_6H_5-NH_2 + NaNO_2 + HCl \rightarrow C_6H_5-N^+ = N.Cl^- + NaCl + H_2O$$

Aniline — Ph diazonium chloride

The above reaction is quantitative under experimental parameters. Therefore, this reaction forms the basis for the estimation of pharmaceutical substances containing a fee primary amino group.

Principle

When sodium nitrite and HCl reacts, they form nitrous acid. This is shown below:

$$NaNO_2 + HCl \longrightarrow NaCl + HNO_2$$

The liberation of iodine from iodide represents the end-point in sodium nitrate titration. The reactions are shown below:

$$KI + HCl \longrightarrow HI + KCl$$

$$2HI + 2HNO_2 \longrightarrow I_2 + 2NO + 2H_2O$$

Small or excess of HNO_2 present at the end-point is detected visually by using starch-iodide paper or paste as an external indicator. The liberated iodine then reacts with starch to form a blue-green colour.

As an alternate method, end-point can be detected amperometrically. Here a pair of bright Pt electrodes are immersed in the titration liquid.

ASSAY METHODS

1. **Preparation of 0.1 M Sodium Nitrite solution:**

   7.5 g of Sodium Nitrite is weighed and dissolved in 1000 ml of distilled water in volumetric flask.

2. **Standardization of 0.1 M Sodium Nitrite solution:**

   Chemicals required:

   Sulphanilamide (previously dried at 105°C for 3 hours): 0.5 g, HCl (11.5 N) – 20 ml, 0.1 M $NaNO_2$ solution.

Principle

Nitrous acid is formed by the treatment of sodium nitrate solution into the acidic reaction mixture. This reacts with the 1° amino group of sulphanilamide quantitatively to form an unstable nitrite. The latter decomposes to form diazonium salt. The diazonium salt thus produced is also unstable, if the reaction mixture is not maintained between 5-10°C. That is, if the temperature is not maintained then the diazonium salt will undergo decomposition to form phenol products. This may react further with nitrous acid.

At the equivalence point, a slight excess of HNO_2 gets detected by employing either starch iodide strip or paste. The reactions may be written as:

$$NaNO_2 + HCl \longrightarrow HNO_2 + NaCl$$

$$H_2NSO_2-C_6H_4-NH_2 + HNO_2 + HCl$$

Sulphanilamide
(172.2)

$$\longrightarrow H_2NSO_2-C_6H_4-N^+ \equiv N.Cl^- + 2H_2O$$

Diazonium salt

$$2I^- + 2HNO_2 + 2H^+ \longrightarrow I_2 + 2NO + 2H_2O$$

Procedure

0.5 g of sulphanilamide is weighed and transferred to a beaker. To this 20 ml of HCl is added followed by 50 ml of distilled water. This is stirred and cooled to 15°C in an ice-bath. 25 g of crushed ice is to be added and then titration with Sodium Nitrite solution is to be done. While titration, stirring is to be done vigorously until the glass – rod tip dipped into the titration solution instantaneously produces a distinct blue ring on getting touched to starch-iodide paper. Each 0.01722 g of Sulphanilamide is equivalent to 1 ml of 0.1 N Sodium Nitrite.

ASSAY OF PHTHALYL SULPHATHIAZOLE

The principle of the assay is based on the following reactions:

$$HOOC-C_6H_4-CONH-C_6H_4-SO_2NH-(C_3H_2NS) \xrightarrow{H_2O} C_6H_4(COOH)_2$$

Pathyalysulphathiazole
(403.43)

Phthalic acid

$$+ H_2O-C_6H_4-SO_2NH-(C_3H_2NS)$$

Sulphathiazole

$$H_2N-C_6H_4-SO_2NH-(C_3H_2NS) + NaNO_2 + 2HCl$$

$$\longrightarrow Cl^-.N \equiv \overset{+}{N}-C_6H_4-SO_2NH-(C_3H_2NS) + NaCl + 2H_2O$$

A diazonium chloride

The above reactions state that Phthalylsulphathiazole undergoes hydrolysis to give phthalic acid and sulphathiazole. The latter reacts quantitatively with nitrous acid to yield the diazonium salt.

Procedure

0.5 g of the sample is weighed. This is heated on a water bath for 2 hours after the addition of 10 ml of NaOH solution. Cool the contents of the flask of 15°C in an ice-bath, add to it 10 ml of water and 20 ml of HCl. Titration is done slowly with 0.1 M $NaNO_2$ solution. Contents of the flask are shaken thoroughly and continuously until a distinct visible blue colour is produced when a drop of the titrated solution is placed on a starch iodide paper. This is 5 minutes after the last addition of 0.1 M $NaNO_2$ solution. When end-point approaches then it is better to add 0.1 M $NaNO_2$ solution at the rate of 0.1 ml.

CHAPTER 9

MISCELLANEOUS ANALYSIS

In this chapter, we shall concentrate on the methods involving estimation of functional groups present in a compound.

Estimation of Amino Groups and Hydroxyl Group

Acetylation

The number of aliphatic and aromatic amino groups and the number of a alcoholic and phenolic hydroxyl groups in an organic compound is determined by acetylation method. This acetylation method is used in analysis of primary and secondary alcohols. Tertiary alcohols cannot be analysed due to its dehydration.

Principle

When sample containing OH group and $-NH_2$ or $-NH$ group is treated with known excess volume of a mixture of acetic anhydride and pyridine (1:3), the reaction occurs. That is, from the acetylating mixture, H of the $-OH$ or $-NH_2$ group is replaced by acetyl group. Pyridine acts as a solvent. It also acts as a catalyst in removing the acidic products by salt formation.

The reactions are summarized as follows:

$$R{-}OH + (CH_3CO)_2O + C_6H_5N \longrightarrow R{-}OCOCH_3 + (C_5H_5\overset{\oplus}{N}H)(CH_3CO\overset{\ominus}{O})$$

$$ArOH + (CH_3CO)_2O + C_6H_5N \longrightarrow ArOCOCH_3 + CH_3COOH$$

$$RNH_2 + (CH_3CO)_2O + C_6H_5N \longrightarrow RNHCOCH_3 + CH_3COOH$$

$$(R)(R_1)NH + (CH_3CO)_2O + C_6H_5N \longrightarrow (R_1)(R_1)N{-}COCH_3 + CH_3COOH$$

When acetylation stops, the unchanged acetic anhydride which remains is hydrolysed by water. Then the total free acetic acid is titrated with standard sodium hydroxide solution.

A blank experiment is performed for necessary correction. The difference in titre value (i.e., in the volume of standard alkali) used in two experiments is the actual amount of acetic acid consumed for acetylating the sample.

Procedure

Two 100 ml round-bottomed flasks are taken and marked as A and B. Both are equipped with water condenser (with $CaCl_2$ guard tube). 0.2 – 0.5 g of sample is taken in flask A followed by addition of 10 ml mixture of acetic anhydride and dry pyridine in 1:3 ratio in both flask A and B. Heat is to be given to both flasks A and B for 1/2 an hour. This procedure is for alcohols but for amines, acetylation is quantitative and occurs at room temperature only. So the reaction mixture is kept for half an hour. Cool to room temperature.

The contents of the flasks are titrated with standard NaOH solution using phenolphthalein as indicator. Difference in vol. of NaOH used in two titrations = acetic acid used in acetylation.

Calculation

Wt. of sample is w g

N_1 = Normality of NaOH solution

V_1 = Volume of NaOH in blank expt.

V_2 = Volume of NaOH in sample

1000 ml of 1 N NaOH = 17.01 g of OH group.

$$(V_1 - V_2) \text{ ml of } N_1 \text{NaOH} = \frac{17.01}{1000} \times (V_1 - V_2) \times N_1 \text{ g of OH group}$$

(let it be x g)

w g of sample contains x g of OH group.

$$\therefore \quad \% \text{ of OH in 100 g sample} = \frac{17.01}{1000} \times (V_1 - V_2) \times \frac{100}{w} \times N_1 \text{ g}$$

Similarly, the formula for calculating the % of amino group in the sample:

$$\% \ NH_2 = \frac{(V_1 - V_2) \times N_1 16.03 \times 100}{w \times 1000}$$

Bromination Method

Both phenol and anilines react with bromine to form bromo derivatives in quantitative yield. Bromine is obtained here by mixing KBr and $KBrO_3$ in dilute HCl.

$$5KBr + KBrO_3 + 6HCl \longrightarrow 3Br_2 + 6KCl + 3H_2O$$

$$\text{Phenol (C}_6\text{H}_5\text{OH)} + 3Br_2 \longrightarrow \text{2,4,6-tribromophenol} + 3HBr$$

$$\text{Aniline (C}_6\text{H}_5\text{NH}_2\text{)} + 3Br_2 \longrightarrow \text{2,4,6-tribromoaniline} + 3HBr$$

The excess of unreacted bromine is treated with Kl. The equivalent iodine so liberated is estimated iodometrically.

$$2KI + Br_2 \longrightarrow 2KBr + I_2$$

$$2Na_2S_2O_3 + I_2 \longrightarrow \underset{\text{Sodium tetrathionate}}{Na_2S_4O_6} + \underset{\text{Sodium iodide}}{2NaI}$$

Procedure

0.25 g of substance is dissolved in 10% NaOH solution (for phenols) or in dilute HCl (for aniline). This is then diluted with 250 ml water in volumetric flask. Pipette out 25 ml of the solution is iodine flask. Add 25 ml of bromate bromide solution; dilute with little water. Add 5 ml concentrate HCl. Stopper the flask shake it for 1 minute. Allow it to stand for ½ an hour with occasional shaking. Cool the iodine flask in ice water. Add 10 ml of 20% Kl solution shake well and keep oxide for some time. Add little water to wash the neck of the stopper.

The liberated iodine is titrated with standard thiosulphate solution using starch as an indicator.

The entire process is repeated to get concordant value perform blank determination and do the necessary correction.

$$\% \text{ purity} = \frac{(V_1 - V_2) \times N_1 \times M \times 100}{W \times 2000 \times Z}$$

V_1 and V_2 = Vol. of (ml) sodium thiosulphate for blank and sample

N_1 = Normality of sodium thiosulphate solution

M = Molecular weight of sample

W = Weight of sample

Z = Number of Br atoms substituted

ILLUSTRATIVE EXAMPLES

1. Aim: Determine the % purity of the given sample of Aniline.

Procedure

0.25 g of aniline is taken in iodine flask. Add 10 ml of 3 N HCl, 25 ml of 0.1 N $KBrO_3$ and 1 g of KBr. Insert the stopper previously moistened with 10% KI solution. Keep it in a dark place for 20 minutes. Shake occasionally. To this add 10 ml of KI solution. Shake well and allow to stand in a dark place for further 10 minutes. The liberated iodine is titrated against N/10 $Na_2S_2O_3$ using starch mucilage solution as indicator. End-point is disappearance of blue colour.

Each ml of N/10 $Na_2S_2O_3$ = 0.01552 g of aniline.

Calculation

T.V. = Blank – Vol. of $Na_2S_2O_3$

% Purity of given sample of Aniline

$$= \frac{\text{T.V.} \times \text{Normality of sod. thiosulphate} \times \text{Eq. factor}}{\text{Wt. taken} \times 0.1 \text{ (Normality of NaOH)}} \times 100$$

= % w/w

Standardization of 0.1 N sodium thiosulphate:

0.49 g of potassium dichromate is weighed and dissolved in distilled water. Transfer to a 100 ml volumetric flask and make up the volume. Pipette out 20 ml of solution and add to it 5 ml of 10% potassium iodate solution and 2 ml concentrate HCl. Titrate against 0.1 N $Na_2S_2O_3$ using starch mucilage as indicator.

$$\text{Normality of } K_2Cr_2O_2 = \frac{\text{Wt. taken} \times 100}{\text{Eq. factor} \times 100}$$

Normality of $K_2Cr_2O_7N_1$ = ... N

Volume of $K_2Cr_2O_7V_1$ = ... ml

Normality of $Na_2S_2O_7N_2$ = ... N

Vol. of $Na_2S_2O_7V_2$ = ... ml

$$V_1N_1 = V_2N_2$$

$$N_2 = \frac{V_1 N_1}{V_2} = \ldots \left(\begin{array}{c}\text{Normality of 0.1 N} \\ \text{Sodium thiosulphate}\end{array}\right)$$

2. Estimation of esters and amides by hydrolysis method:

Ester and amide functional group are estimated by hydrolysis with standard alkali. As compared to esters, amide hydrolysis needs heating with stronger alkali for long period of time.

$$RCOOC_2H_5 + NaOH \longrightarrow RCOONa + C_2H_5OH$$

$$RCONH_2 + NaOH \longrightarrow RCOONa + NH_3$$

Procedure

0.8-1.3 g of substance is taken in a round bottomed flask. Round bottom flask is equipped with a water condenser 50 ml of standard alkali solution is added N/2 NaOH solution is used for esters and 2 N NaOH is needed for amides. Aqueous solution is needed for water soluble substances and alcoholic solution is needed for water insoluble substances.

This reaction mixture is to be heated under reflex condition. Time duration for reflux is half an hour for esters and 3 hours for amides. Completion of reflux is indicated by the disappearance of purity odour of the ester. For amides, it is the expulsion of ammonia which indicates the end of reaction. Cool the round bottomed flask. Then at room temperature, transfer the contents of round bottomed flask into 250 ml of volumetric flask. Dilute with distilled water upto the mark. The unreacted alkali is determined by titrating with standard acid. For the same, 25 ml of this dilute solution is taken and is titrated against standard acid. The strength of acid to be taken is N/10 HCl for esters and 2 N HCl for amides. Phenolphthalein solution is used as indicator.

Calculation

For esters

Let the wt. of substance = W g

Amount alkali taken in RB flask = 50 ml of N/2 NaOH

= 25 ml of N NaOH = V_1

Amount of alkali is equivalent to 10 V_2 of N/2 HCl or V_2 ml of N HCl

Amount of alkali used in hydrolysis = $(25 - V_2)$ ml of N NaOH

∴ 1 mole of alkali = 1 mole of ester

1000 ml of N alkali = 1 mole of ester (M)

$$\text{Amount of ester in sample} = \frac{M \times (V_1 - V_2)}{1000}$$

For amides,

$$\text{Amount of amide in sample} = \frac{M \times (100 - 10V_2)}{1000}$$

2 N HCl is used for titration.

3. Aim: To determine the percentage purity of the given sample of Methyl Salicylate.

Principle

Methyl salicylate is estimated by back titration method. Phenolphthalein solution is used as an indicator. Methyl salicylate on treatment with a known quantity of sodium hydroxide is hydrolysed to yield sodium salicylate. The excess of alkali remained is back titrated with std. HCl.

Blank titration is performed without the sample. This is for the necessary correction. The latter involves the difference between the two titrations (blank is without sample and the other titre value) provide the actual amount of alkali required for given ester.

[Reaction scheme: o-HO–C_6H_4–$OCOCH_3$ $\xrightarrow{NaOH}$ o-HO–C_6H_4–COOH $\xrightarrow{NaOH}$ o-HO–C_6H_4–COONa]

$$NaOH + HCl \longrightarrow NaCl + H_2O$$

Procedure

0.5 g of Methyl salicylate is taken. It is dissolved in 25 ml alcohol. Add 1 drop of phenol red solution. This is then neutralised with 0.4 N NaCH solution. To the neutralized solution add 50 ml of 0.1 N NaOH and reflux it on a water-bath for 30 minutes cool. Titrate it with 0.1 N

HCl using Phenol red as indicator. Perform blank titration and do necessary correction.

Each ml of 0.1 N NaOH is equivalent to 0.01522 g of Methyl Salicylate.

Calculations

I. Standardization of 0.1 N sodium hydroxide

Wt. of the bottle + sample =

Wt. of the bottle + sample after transferring =

Wt. of sample =

Potassium Hydrogen Phthalate Vs 0.1 N Sodium Hydroxide

S. No.	Content of Flask	Burette reading		Vol. of NaOH	Indi-cator	End-point
		Initial	Final			
1.	0.5 g of pot. hydrogen-phthalate + 25 ml H_2O + 1 – 2 drops of phenolph-thalein	0 ml	X ml	X ml	Phenolphthalein	Pale Pink Colour

Normality of sodium hydroxide

$$= \frac{\text{Wt. taken}}{\text{T.V.} \times \text{Eq. factor}}$$

= ..... N

II. Standardisation of 0.1 N Hydrochloric acid 0.1 N Sodium Hydroxide Vs 0.1 N Hydrochloric acid

S. No.	Content of Flask	Burette reading		Vol. of HCl	Indicator	End-point
		Initial	Final			
1.	20 ml NaOH (0.1 N) + 1 drop phenolphthalein solution	0 ml	X_1 ml	X_1 ml	Phenolphthalein	Disappearance pale pink colour

$$\text{Vol. of sodium hydroxide } V_1 = X \text{ ml}$$

$$\text{Normality of hydroxide } N_1 = \text{.....} \text{ N}$$

$$\text{Vol. of HCl } V_2 = X_1 \text{ ml}$$

$$\text{Normality of HCl } N_2 = \text{.....} \text{ N}$$

$$V_1N_1 = V_2N_2$$

$$N_2 = \frac{V_1 N_1}{V_2} = \text{.....} \text{ N}$$

Assay of Methyl Salicylate

Wt. of bottle + sample =

Wt. of bottle + sample after transferring =

Wt. of sample =

Excess alkali (Methyl salicylate) Vs 0.1 N Hydrochloric acid

S. No.	Content of Flask	Burette reading		Vol. of HCl	Indicator	End-point
		Initial	Final			
1.	Sample + 25 ml alcohol + 50 ml NaOH	0 ml	.... ml	ml	Phenol red	App. of Yellow colour
2.	25 ml alcohol + 50 ml NaOH sol.	0 ml	.... ml	ml		Disapp. of pale pink colour

Vol. conversion (Y) = Blank – T.V. = ... ml

$$\left.\begin{array}{r}\text{\% purity of}\\ \text{Me Salicylate}\end{array}\right\} = \frac{\text{Y} \times \text{Normality of HCl} \times \text{Eq. Factor} \times 100}{\text{Wt. taken} \times 0.1}$$

= ..... % w/w

Estimation of Carbonyl Groups

(i) Hydroxylamine hydrochloride – pyridine method

Principle

When a weighed quantity of carbonyl compound is treated with excess of hydroxylamine hydrochloride in the presence of pyridine, it yields oxime. Pyridine hydrochloride so formed is estimated with standard sodium hydroxide solution.

$$R_2C{=}O + H_2NOH.HCl \rightleftharpoons R_2C{=}N.OH + HCl + H_2O$$

$$C_6H_5N.HCl + NaOH \longrightarrow C_6H_5N + NaCl + H_2O$$

Procedure

A mixture of 30 ml hydroxylamine hydrochloride and 100 ml of bromophenol blue solution is taken in a 250 ml Iodine flask. To this accurately weighed carbonyl compound is added. Stopper it and allow it to stand at room temperature for ½ an hour.

For ketones and other hindered aldehydes, refluxing of the mixture on a boiling water bath is needed for more than 2 hours for complete reaction.

Titrate the contents of the flask with 0.5 N NaOH solution till end-point of blue-green colour. Perform blank titration and do necessary correction.

Calculations

Wt. of carbonyl sample = W g

Normality of NaOH solution = N

Vol. of std. NaOH used in blank expt. = V_1

Vol. of std. NaOH used in sample expt. = V

Mol. Wt. of sample = M

$$\% \text{ carbonyl group} = \frac{(V - V_1) \times N \times M \times 100}{W \times 100}$$

(ii) Preparation of Reagents

(a) **Hydroxylamine HCl solution:** 17.5 g of sample is diluted with water and dilute it with 500 ml EtOH.

(b) **Bromophenol blue indicator solution:** 4% alcoholic solution of bromophenol (1 ml) in pure pyridine (5 ml) is taken and is diluted to 250 ml with ethanol.

(c) **Methanolic sodium hydroxide solution (0.5 N):** 5 mg of sodium hydroxide pellets are dissolved in 25 ml water. This is taken in a volumetric flask and volume is made upto the mark with absolute methanol. It is standardized with 0.5 N HCl using bromophenol blue as indicator.

(d) **Hydrazone formation method:** It is an example of gravimetric method. The principle involves reaction of aldehydes and ketones with 2, 4-dinitrophenyl hydrazine to produce phenyl hydrazones. Quantitative determination of the carbonyl group is completed by taking weight of the hydrazone so formed.

Procedure

50 ml of 2, 4-dinitrophenyl hydrazine is taken in a 250 ml glass stoppered conical flask. Accurately weighed quantity of sample, i.e., 0.02 – 0.04 millimole is added to it. The contents of the flask is shaken until a clear solution is obtained. This is allowed to stand on an ice-bath for an hour with occasional shaking. The precipitate is to be filtered via previously dried and constant weighed sintered glass G_3 crucible. It is to be washed with a few ml of 2 N HCl and water successively. It is to be dried at constant weight at 100-105°C.

Calculations

Wt. of sample = W g

Wt. of hydrazone = obtained = W g

$$\% \text{ of purity} = \frac{W \times f \times 100}{W}$$

$$f \text{ (gravimetric factor)} = \frac{\text{Mol. wt. of carbonyl compound}}{\text{Mol. wt. of hydrazone}}$$

(iii) Determination of formaldehyde (Romijn's Iodometric method)

Formaldehyde is obtained as formation which contains 35% by weight of formaldehyde. This method is based on treatment of formaldehyde with excess of iodine solution in alkaline medium. As a result, HCHO (formaldehyde) gets oxidized to HCOOH (formic acid).

The equation is:

$$HCHO + I_2 + 3NaOH \longrightarrow HCOONa + 2NaI + 2H_2O$$

Sodium hypoiodite oxidizes HCHO to HCOOH:

The unused NaOI is determined iodometrically on adding HCl, following reaction takes place.

$$NaOI + NaI + 2HCl \longrightarrow 2NaCl + H_2O + I_2$$

The liberated iodine is titrated with a standard $Na_2S_2O_6$ solution to form sodium tetrathionate.

$$2Na_2S_2O_3 + I_2 \longrightarrow 2NaI + \underset{\text{Sodium tetrathionate}}{Na_2S_4O_6}$$

Blank titration is done for necessary correction. That is, the difference between sample titre and blank titre gives the amount of iodine which reacted with the formaldehyde sample. Hence, knowing the amount of iodine consumed, the actual amount of HCHO can be determined. That calculation is as follows:

$$2Na_2S_2O_3 \equiv I_2 \equiv HCHO \ (= 30 \text{ g } HCHO)$$

M.W. of HCHO = 30

$$Na_2S_2O_3 \equiv \tfrac{1}{2} I_2 \equiv \tfrac{1}{2} \text{HCHO} (= 15 \text{ g HCHO})$$

$$1000 \text{ ml of } 1 \text{ N } Na_2S_2O_3 \equiv 15 \text{ g HCHO}$$

$$1000 \text{ ml of } 0.1 \text{ N } Na_2S_2O_3 \equiv 1.5 \text{ g HCHO}$$

$$1 \text{ ml of } 0.1 \text{ N } Na_2S_2O_3 \equiv 0.0015 \text{ g HCHO} (= 1.5 \text{ mg HCHO})$$

Procedure

0.1 g of formalin is taken into a 250 ml volumetric flask. It is diluted with distilled water to the mark. Mix thoroughly 25 ml of this solution is taken into a 250 ml iodine flask. To this add 50 ml 0.1 N I_2 solution. Add 2 N NaOH dropwise with constant stirring until pale yellow colour appears.

Blank titration is performed by taking the same ml of 0.1 N I_2 solution and NaOH std. solution is added dropwise without the sample.

After 10-15 minutes, contents of both the flasks are acidified by adding excess of 4 N HCl solution. The liberated iodine is titrated with 0.1 N $Na_2S_2O_3$ solution using starch mucilage as indicator.

Calculation

Blank titre = y ml

Sample titre = x ml

Normality of $Na_2S_2O_3$ sol. = 0.1 N

Wt. of formalin = W g 25 ml of sample solution is taken

(y – x) ml = I_2 consumed by sample in terms of 0.1 N $Na_2S_2O_3$

$$1 \text{ ml of } 0.1 \text{ N } Na_2S_2O_3 \equiv 0.0015 \text{ g HCHO}$$

$$\therefore (y - x) \text{ ml of } 0.1 \text{ N } Na_2S_2O_3 \equiv (y - x) \times 0.0015 \text{ g HCHO}$$

$$\text{W g of sample contains } \frac{(y - x) \times 0.0015}{W} \text{ g HCHO}$$

$$100 \text{ g of sample contains } \frac{(y - x) \times 0.0015}{W} \times 100 \text{ g HCHO}$$

$$\% \text{ HCHO} = \frac{(y - x) \times 0.0015 \times 100}{W}$$

(iv) Determination of Acetone by Messinger's iodometric method

Principle

Acetone reacts with I_2 in the presence of alkali as per the equation:

$$CH_3COCH_3 + 3I_2 + 4NaOH \longrightarrow CHI_3 + CH_3COONa + 3NaI + 3H_2O$$

$$CH_3COCH_3 \cong 3I_2$$

$$I_2 \cong 2Na_2S_2O_3$$

$$6Na_2S_2O_3 \equiv 3I_2 \equiv CH_3COCH_3$$

$$Na_2S_2O_3 \equiv ½\ I_2 \equiv 1/6\ CH_3COCH_3$$

$$\text{M.W. } CH_3COCH_3 = 58.081$$

$\therefore$ 1000 ml of 1 N $Na_2S_2O_3 \equiv 1/6 \times 58.081$ (= 9.680 g CH_3COCH_3)

1 ml of 0.1 N $Na_2S_2O_3 \equiv$ 9.680 g acetone.

Procedure

0.001-0.025 g acetone is taken in an iodine flask. Add 200 ml distilled water. Add 25 ml of 1 N NaOH solution. Shake well. Keep for 5 minutes. Titrate it with 0.1 N I_2 solution till end-point.

Perform blank titration and do necessary correction. Acidify the contents of the flask with excess of HCl. The liberated iodine is titrated with standard $Na_2S_2O_3$ solution.

Calculation

Blank T.V. = y ml

Sample T.V. = x ml

Normality of $Na_2S_2O_3$ = 0.1 N

Amount of iodine consumed is (y – x) ml of 0.1 N $Na_2S_2O_3$ solution.

1 ml of 0.1 N $Na_2S_2O_3$ solution $\equiv$ 0.9680 mg of acetone

(y – x) ml of 0.1 N $Na_2S_2O_3$ solution = (y – x) × 0.9680 mg acetone

$\therefore$ The sample will contain (y – x) × 0.9680 mg of acetone

Determination of Carboxylic acid group:

The number of carboxyl group present in an acid is equal to the basicity of the molecule.

Example: CH_3COOH is a monobasic acid (Acetic acid)

$(CH.OH.COOH)_2$ is a dibasic acid (Tartaric acid)

The formula is:

$$\text{Basicity} = \frac{\text{No. of COOH group}}{\text{Molecule}} = \frac{\text{Mol. wt.}}{\text{Eq. wt.}}$$

(v) Determination of Equivalent Weight of an Acid by Iodometric Method

This method is based on preparation of a known quantity of solution of carboxylic acid sample. 10 ml of this solution is taken in an iodine flask. It is treated with KI and KIO_3. It is stoppered and kept for 10-15 minutes. Occasional shaking is needed. The liberated iodine is titrated with a standard solution of $Na_2S_2O_3$ using starch mucilage as indicator.

Calculate the amount of acid that would be equivalent to 1000 ml of 1 M $Na_2S_2O_3$ solution. This amount is equivalent weight of carboxylic acid.

$$6RCOOH + 5KI + KIO_3 \longrightarrow 6RCOOK + 3H_2O + 3I_2$$

$$3I_2 + 6Na_2S_2O_3 \longrightarrow 3Na_2S_4O_6 + 6\ NaI$$

$$6RCOOH \equiv 3I_2 \equiv 6Na_2S_2O_3$$

$$Na_2S_2O_3 \equiv RCOOH$$

$$1000 \text{ ml of } 1 \text{ M } Na_2S_2O_3 \equiv 1 \text{ g eq. of acid.}$$

Procedure

Weigh 0.48 g of carboxylic acid and dissolve it in water. Make the solution upto 100 ml with distilled water. Take 10 ml of this solution in iodine flask. Add 3 g of KIO_3 and 3 g of KI. Keep the iodine flask well stoppered for 10-15 minutes. The liberated iodine is titrated with 0.05 M $Na_2S_2O_3$ solution, T.V. = 16 ml. Calculate equivalent weight of acid.

$$10 \text{ ml of acid} = 16 \text{ ml of } 0.05 \text{ M } Na_2S_2O_3$$

$$100 \text{ ml of acid} = 160 \text{ ml of } 0.05 \text{ M } Na_2S_2O_3$$

$$0.48 \text{ g of acid} = 80 \text{ ml of } 0.1 \text{ M } Na_2S_2O_3$$

$$0.48 \text{ g of acid} = 80 \text{ ml of } 0.1 \text{ M } Na_2S_2O_3$$

$$0.48 \text{ g acid} = 8 \text{ ml of } 1 \text{ M } Na_2S_2O_3$$

$$8 \text{ ml of } 1 \text{ M } Na_2S_2O_3 \cong 0.48 \text{ g acid}$$

$$1000 \text{ ml of } 1 \text{ M } Na_2S_2O_3 = \frac{0.48}{8} \times 1000 = 60 \text{ g acid}$$

$\therefore$ Eq. Wt. of acid = 60

Let, Molecular weight = 60

$$\text{Number of COOH groups} = \frac{\text{M.W.}}{\text{E.W.}} = \frac{60}{60} = 1$$

Determination of Glucose

Glucose determination is based on its reaction with Fehling's solution at high temperature.

Preparation of reagents

(i) **Preparation of std. glucose solution:**

Weigh 1.25 g of pure anhydrous glucose dissolve it in distilled water to make upto 250 ml. It is used to standardize Fehlings solution.

(ii) **Preparation of std. Fehling's solution:**

Solution A: 6.93 g of pure $CuSO_4.5H_2O$ is dissolved in distilled water. Volume is made up to 100 ml in volume flask.

Solution B: 34.6 g of crystalline sodium potassium tartrate is weighed. Its formula is $C_4H_4O_6Na\ K.4H_2O$. It is dissolved in warm water. Weigh 12 g of NaOH and dissolve it in little quantity of distilled water. Mix both the solutions and make up the volume upto 100 ml in volume flask.

Procedure

25 ml of Fehling's solution is taken in a conical flask. To this 25 ml of distilled water is added. It is heated to boil. Glucose solution is added from burette. After each addition, the red coloured cuprous oxide is

allowed to settle down. Disappearance of blue colour in supernatent liquid is observed. The temperature of titration flask decreases during observation. Hence, it should be re-heated. End-point of titration is the disappearance of blue colour in the supernatent liquid. Titration is to be repeated for concordant reading.

Procedure for determination of concentration of given glucose solution

25 ml of Fehling's solution is taken in a conical flask. It is titrated with the given solution of glucose. This procedure is similar to that of standardization of Fehling's solution.

Calculations

25 ml of Fehling's solution $\equiv$ 24.5 ml of std. glucose solution

25 ml of Fehling's solution $\equiv$ 26.7 ml of test glucose solution

$$\therefore \left.\begin{array}{c}\text{Strength of given}\\ \text{glucose solution}\end{array}\right\} = \text{Strength of std. glucose solution} \times \frac{24.5}{26.7}$$

250 ml of std. glucose solution contains 1.25 g glucose

1000 ml of std. glucose solution contains $\frac{1.25}{250} \times 1000 = 5$ g glucose/lit.

$$\therefore \left.\begin{array}{c}\text{Strength of given}\\ \text{glucose solution}\end{array}\right\} = \frac{5 \times 24.5}{26.5} = 4.59 \text{ g/l}$$

CHAPTER 10

ILLUSTRATIVE EXAMPLES

This Chapter gives illustrative examples of the Assay of Pharmaceutical Inorganic Substances. Assay is done by Titrimetric Analysis. The latter is a method of determining quantities of component substances in a sample by measure. Here standard solution of reagent called as titrant is added from a purette to a solution of the substance present in conical flask for determining its quantity. That is, the quantity of the substance present in the flask.

Addition of titrant to conical flask is continued till both the substances reach chemical equivalent point. This point is called as equivalence point or stoichiometric point. The latter is the end-point of titration.

End-point is detected in the ways:

(a) Physical change like precipitation.

(b) Appearance of colour by titrant, e.g., $KMnO_4$ solution.

(c) Use of indicator (it causes a colour change in the solution being titrated when the reaction completes).

Pharmacopoeial assays of drugs employ the following types of titrations:

(a) Acidimetry and Alkalimetry

(b) Oxidation-Reduction titration

(c) Precipitation titration

(d) Complexometric titration

(e) Non-aqueous titration.

1. Assay of Sodium Bicarbonate

Procedure

1 g of sample is dissolved in 20 ml water and titrated with 0.5 N sulphuric acid using Methyl orange solution as indicator. Colour change at end-point occurs which is from yellow to pink.

The reaction at equivalence point is acidic due to the formation of carbonic acid (H_2CO_3). H_2CO_3 forms by interaction of CO_2 and H_2O.

1000 ml of N/2 H_2SO_4 is equivalent to ½ $NaHCO_3$

Each ml of 0.5 N H_2SO_4 is equivalent to 0.042 g of $NaHCO_3$

$$\% \text{ purity of } NaHCO_3 = \frac{V \times N \times 0.042 \times 100}{0.5 \times W}$$

V = Vol. of acid (T.V.)

N = Normality of acid

W = Wt. of sample

2. Assay of Sodium Carbonate

Procedure

2 g of substance is dissolved in 20 ml of distilled water. It is titrated with 0.5 N H_2SO_4 using bromophenol blue solution as indicator.

Colour change at end-point is from blue-violet to yellow. Like the previous assays, end-point is acidic. It is due to formation of H_2CO_3. Indicator is selected in such a way which will show colour change in acidic pH. The pH range of bromophenol blue is 2.8-4.6.

1000 ml of N/2 sulphuric acid is equivalent to ½ $NaCO_3.10H_2O$

Each ml of 0.5 N sulphuric acid is equivalent to 0.07154 g of $Na_2CO_3.10H_2O$

$$\% \text{ purity of } Na_2CO_3 = \frac{V \times N \times 0.07154 \times 100}{0.5 \times W}$$

V = Vol. of acid (Titre value T.V.)

N = Normality of acid

W = wt. of Na_2CO_3 taken of assay

3. Assay of Strong Ammonia Solution

Assay is based on back titration method. It is because ammonia is volatile in nature, so some amount of it gets lost during titration. A known amount of solution is treated with excess of std. H_2SO_4. The unreacted excess acid is back titrated with std. alkali. Methyl red is used as indicator. End-point is change in colour from yellow to red.

$$2NH_3 + H_2SO_4 \longrightarrow (NH_4)_2\ SO_4$$

Procedure

3 g sample is placed in a conical flask having 50 ml of 1 N H_2SO_4. Excess of acid is back titrated with 1 N NaOH using Me red solution as indicator.

Each ml of 1 N H_2SO_4 is equivalent to 0.01703 g of NH_3

1000 ml of N/1 H_2SO_4 is equivalent to NH_3

$$\% \text{ purity} = \frac{[(V_1 \times N_1) - (V_2 \times N_2)] \times 0.01703}{1 \times W} \times 100$$

V_1 = Vol. of acid

N_1 = Normality of acid

V_2 = Vol. of alkali

N_2 = Normality of alkali

W = Wt. of sample

Oxidation Reduction Titration

1. Assay of Hydrogen Peroxide Solution

Procedure

Dilute 10 ml of hydrogen peroxide solution to 250 ml with distilled water. From this, 25 ml of solution is taken and 5 ml of 5 N H_2SO_4 is added. This is done in conical flask. This solution is the titrated with 0.1 N $KMnO_4$. End-point is appearance of permanent pink colour.

$$2H_2O_2 \longrightarrow 2H_2O + O_2$$

$$68.04 \text{ g of } H_2O_2 \equiv 22400 \text{ ml } O_2$$

(Vol. strength of solution is the number of ml of oxygen at N.T.P. that can be obtained by complete thermal decomposition of 1 ml of solution.)

$$\therefore \quad 68.04 \text{ g } H_2O_2 \equiv 22400 \text{ ml } O_2$$

$$1 \text{ g } H_2O_2 \equiv 329.2 \text{ ml } O_2$$

Our test sample contains 5.4% w/v H_2O_2

$$\therefore \quad 100 \text{ ml sample} \equiv 5.40 \text{ g } H_2O_2$$

$$1 \text{ ml sample} \equiv 0.0540 \text{ g } H_2O_2$$

$$\equiv 0.0540 \text{ g} \times 329.2 \text{ ml } O_2$$

$$\equiv 17.77 \text{ ml } O_2$$

$\therefore$ Vol. strength of our sample is 17.77 ml.

Each ml of 0.1 N $KMnO_4$ is equivalent to 0.0001701 g of H_2O_2

Calculations

$$\% \text{ purity (w/v)} = \frac{V_1 \times N \times 0.001701 \times 10}{0.1 \times V_2} \times 100$$

V_1 = T.V. (Vol. of $KMnO_4$ consumed)

N = Normality of $KMnO_4$

V_2 = Vol. of sample taken

2. Assay of Copper Sulphate

Principle

It is based on iodometric titration method. Here, reaction occurs between salt and KI in presence of acetic acid to form cupric iodide (CuI_2). CuI_2 is unstable and gets converted to cuprous iodide (Cu_2I_2) and iodine. The liberated iodine is titrated with std. sodium thiosulphate solution using starch solution as indicator. Indicator is added later. When blue colour of solution disappears then potassium thiocyanate is added and titration is consumed till end-point of the reaction. Decomposition of cupric iodide to cuprous iodide and iodine takes place which is reversible process. Soluble thiocyanate makes the reaction quantitative. Potassium thiocyanate is added at the end of reaction to prevent adsorption of iodine by cuprous thiocyanate.

$$2CuSO_4 + 4KI \longrightarrow 2\,CuI_2 + 2K_2SO_4$$

$$2CuI_2 \rightleftharpoons Cu_2I_2 + I_2$$

$$I_2 + 2Na_2S_2O_3 \longrightarrow Na_2S_4O_6 + 2NaI$$

$$2CuSO_4.5H_2O_3 \equiv I_2 \equiv 2e$$

1000 ml of 0.1 N $Na_2S_2O_3$ is equivalent to 0.02497 g $CuSO_4.5H_2O$

Procedure

1 g of a sample is dissolved in 50 ml of distilled water. 3 g of KI and 5 ml of acetic acid is added. The liberated iodine is titrated with 0.1 N $Na_2S_2O_3$ using starch solution as indicator. Titration is to be continued till faint blue colour is obtained. Then add 2 g KCNS. Stir well. Titration is to be continued till disappearance of blue colour.

Calculations

$$\%\ \text{purity} = \frac{\text{T.V.} \times \text{N} \times 0.02497}{0.1 \times \text{W}} \times 100$$

T.V. = Titre value

N = Normality of sodium thiosulphate solution

W = Wt. of copper sulphate sample taken for assay.

Precipitation Titration

Quantitative precipitation is a technique employed in titrimetric analysis. It is possible to determine the point at which precipitation gets completed.

Example: $AgNO_3 + NaCl \longrightarrow AgCl \downarrow + NaNO_3$

Here chloride ion of sodium chloride is estimated by reaction with silver nitrate. So quantitative amount of silver chloride is ppted. by quantitative amount of silver nitrate and sodium chloride.

Titration which involve use of standard solution of silver nitrate is known as Argentimetric titration.

Examples:

1. Assay of sodium chloride injection by Mohr's Method

Procedure

Weigh 0.25 g of sodium chloride and dissolve it in 50 ml of water taken in a conical flask. This is then titrated with 0.1 N silver nitrate using potassium chromate as indicator.

$$\% \text{ purity (w/v)} = \frac{V_1 \times N \times 0.005845}{0.1 \times V_2} \times 100$$

V_1 = Vol. of silver nitrate

N = Normality of silver nitrate solution

V_2 = Vol. of sample taken

∴ Std. of N silver nitrate solution.

2. Assay of silver chloride injection by Volhard's Method

Principle

A definite quantity of sample is diluted with water. This is treated with measured vol. of std. silver nitrate solution in the presence of nitric acid and nitrobenzene. The excess of silver nitrate is titrated with std. ammonium thiocyanate solution. Ferric ammonium sulphate is used as an indicator.

$$NaCl + AgNO_3 \longrightarrow AgCl + NaNO_3$$

$$AgNO_3 + NH_4SCN \longrightarrow AgSCN + NH_4NO_3$$

1000 ml of 0.1 N $AgNO_3$ is equivalent to 1/10 NaCl

1000 ml of 0.1 N $AgNO_3$ is equivalent to 0.005844 g NaCl

Procedure

Take vol. of NaCl equal to 0.25 g in a conical flask or glass stoppered flask. To this add 50 ml distilled water. Add 50 ml of 0.1 N $AgNO_3$, 3 ml HNO_3, 5 ml nitrobenzene and 2 ml of ferric ammonium sulphate. Shake well. This is to be titrated with 0.1 N NH_4SCN. End-point is appearance of reddish yellow colour.

$$\% \text{ purity (w/v)} = \frac{(V_1 \times N_1) - (V_2 \times N_2) \times 0.005844}{0.1 \times V_3} \times 100$$

V_1 = Vol. of $AgNO_3$ solution

N_1 = Normality of $AgNO_3$ solution

V_2 = Vol. of NH_4SCN solution (T.V.)

N_2 = Normality of NH_4SCN solution

V_3 = Vol. of NaCl sample

Complexometric Titration

1. Assay of Magnesium Sulphate

Principle

Assay is based on titration with 0.05 M disodium ethylenediamine tetraacetate using mordant black 11 mixture as indicator. Ammonia buffer solution is added to maintain pH 10. End-point is appearance of blue colour.

Reaction is as follows

$$Mg^{2+} + [H_2X]^{2-} \longrightarrow \underset{\text{Anion of disod. ethylenediamine tetraacetate}}{[MgX]^{2-}} + 2H^+$$

1000 ml of 0.05 M disodium ethylenediamine tetraacetate is equivalent to 1/20 $MgSO_4$.

Procedure

0.3 g of sample is dissolved in 50 ml water. 10 ml of strong NH_3 – NH_4Cl solution is added. It is titrated with 0.05 M disodium ethylenediamine tetraacetate. 0.1 g of Mordant black 11 mixture is used as indicator. Titration is to be continued till the discharged of pink colour. End-point is appearance of blue colour.

$$\% \text{ purity} = \frac{\text{T.V.} \times M \times 0.00602}{0.05 \times W} \times 100$$

M = Actual molarity of titrant

W = Wt. of sample taken

Preparation of strong NH_3–NH_4Cl solution buffer:

Take 67.5 g of NH_4Cl in 740 ml of strong NH_3 solution. Add distill water to make upto 1000 ml.

2. Assay of Calcium Carbonate

Procedure

0.1 g sample is dissolved in 3 ml of dilute HCl and 10 ml water. This is to be boiled for 10 mins. Cool, dilute to 50 ml with water. Titrate this mixture with 0.05 M disodium ethylenediamine tetraacetate. Titrate till few ml is left for expect end-point. Then add 8 ml of NaOH solution and 0.1 g of calcon mixture. Titration is to be continued till colour changes from pink to full blue colour.

Each ml of 0.05 M disodium ethylenediamine tetraacetate is equivalent to 0.005004 g of $CaCO_3$.

Calculation

$$\% \text{ purity} = \frac{V \times M \times 0.005004}{0.05 \times W} \times 100$$

V = Vol. of titrant

M = Molarity of titrant

W = Wt. of sample

Preparation of 0.05 M disodium edetate

18.6 g of disodium ethylene diamine tetraacetate is dissolved in 1000 ml water. This is 0.05 M solution.

Std. of 0.05 M disod. edetate:

1.251 g of $CaCO_3$ is added to 250 ml std. flask.

Add dil. HCl to dissolve $CaCO_3$. Boil off excess CO_2. Cool make up the volume. Pipette 20 ml of this solution to conical flask. Add 5 ml NH_3–NH_4Cl buffer. Add Mordant Black II mixtures as indicator. The contents of this conical flask is titrated with 0.05 M disod. edetate till pink colour changes to blue. A blank titration is done for necessary correction.

Strength of 0.05 M disodium edetate

$$= \frac{\text{Wt. of } CaCO_3 \times 20}{(T.V. - B.V.) \times 0.005004 \times 250} = ... M$$

Methods of Gravimetric Analysis

1. Gravimetric Determination of Barium as Barium Sulphate

The determination is based on the following reaction:

$$Ba^{2+} + SO_4^{2-} \longrightarrow BaSO_4 \text{ white ppt.}$$

Procedure

1. Repeated heating at 500-600°C, cooling and weighing to get the constant wt. of porcelain or silica crucible is to be done.
2. The solid sample is to be dried. Accurately weighed portion of sample is taken in beaker. It is dissolved in distilled water. For liquid sample, definite vol. is to be taken in beaker.
3. To this sample add 5 ml of dilute HCl followed by addition of 150 ml water.
4. Heat this solution 80°C. Then add an excess of hot dilute H_2SO_4 via a glass rod. This mixture is stirred thoroughly for 2-3 minutes. This is done because at high T, colloidal particles coagulate to form bigger particles. The bigger particles are easily filtered.

5. In order to test complete precipitation, a few drops of dilute H_2SO_4 is added to the supernatant solution.
6. Whatmann filter paper number 40 is fitted properly in a funnel. The supernatent liquid is poured through it. The filtrate is collected in beaker ppt. is first washed with hot water containing a few drops of dilute H_2SO_4. Then it is washed with distilled water to remain the acid. In order to check the filtrate from lack of ppt. or turbidity, it is to be treated with silver nitrate.

   Then this ppt. is fully transferred to a filter paper.
7. After transferring all ppt. to filter paper, it is folded. This is then placed in a porcelain or a silica crucible whose constant weight is to be determined.
8. The ppt. is loosely covered and slowly heated. The filter paper chars (turns black). Volatile matter gets expelled out.
9. After completion of charring, temperature is increased crucible becomes fully red. Crucible is partially covered with lid so that air can enter it.
10. If ppt. is not white then it is cooled. Add a drop of diluted H_2SO_4. Ppt. is then strongly heated to red-heat for 10-15 minutes. The crucible is cooled in air for 2-3 minutes. Then it is transferred to a desiccator. Here again it is cooled for 15 minutes weight is taken at this stage.
11. Weight of the ppt. is multiplied by gravimetric factor (f)

∴ Wt. of substance sought is

$$= \text{Wt. of ppt.} \times \frac{\text{Formula wt. of substance (a) sought}}{\text{Formula wt. of substance (b) weighed}}$$

$$= W \times \frac{\text{Formula. wt. of Ba}}{\text{Formula. wt. of } BaSO_4}$$

$$f = \frac{\text{Formula wt. of substance (a) sought}}{\text{Formula wt. of substance (b) weighed}}$$

2. Gravimetric determination of Sulphate as Barium Sulphate

Procedure

It is same as above. The ppt. of $BaSO_4$ is filtered, washed, dried and weighed.

Formula wt. of $BaSO_4 = 233.42$

Formula wt. of SO_4^{2-} ion = 96.06

$$\left.\begin{array}{l}\therefore \text{The chemical factor} \\ \text{for conversion of } BaSO_4 \\ \text{to } SO_4^{2-} \text{ ion}\end{array}\right\} = \frac{96.06}{233.42} = 0.4115$$

∴ Wt. of $BaSO_4 \times 0.4115$ is = Qty. of SO_4^- ions present in the given amount of sample.

Non-Aqueous Titration

1. Assay of Fenfluramine HCl I.P.

Procedure

0.3 g of sample is weighed. Proceed as per Method A for Non-Aqueous Titration. Refer Appendix 3.45 of I.P. 1996. Determine end-point potentiometrically. Perform blank determination to make necessary correction.

Each ml of 0.1 M perchloric acid is equivalent to 0.02677 g of $C_{12}H_{16}F_3N$. HCl.

2. Assay of Metronidazole I.P.

150 mg of sample is dissolved in 50 ml of anhydrous glacial AcOH and proceed as per I.P. 96. Carry method A for non-aqueous titatration (NAT) appendix 3.45 of I.P. 1996. End point is determined potentiometrically. Perform blank titration and do necessary correction. Each ml of 0.1 M perchloric acid is equivalent to 0.01712 g of $C_6H_9N_3O_3$.

3. Assay of Acetazolomide I.P.

Procedure

400 mg of sample is dissolved in 90 ml of dimethyl formamide. Proceed as per Method A for NAT. Appendix 3.45 of I.P. 1996 using

0.1 M tetrabutyl ammonium hydroxide as titrant. End-point is determined potentiometrically. Perform blank titration to make necessary correction. Each ml of 0.1 M tetrabutyl-ammonium hydroxide is equivalent to 0.02222 g of $C_4H_6N_4O_3S_2$.

4. Assay of Gatifloxacin

Procedure

To the conical flask, add weighed quantity of sample. Then add 40 ml glacial AcOH.

Crystal violet indicator is added. Titrate with 0.1 M perchloric acid till colour change.

$$\% \text{ Purity} = \frac{V \times \text{dm Eq} \times 100}{m}$$

V = T.V. (ml of 0.1 M $HClO_4$ used)

dm Eq = decimiliequivalent of Gatifloxacin

m = wt. of sample taken

Blank determination is done for correction purpose.

BIBLIOGRAPHY

1. Bentley and Driver's; Textbook of Pharmaceutical Chemistry, 8th Edition, OUP, New Delhi.
2. Textbook of Pharmaceutical Analysis, 3rd Edition, Dr. S. Ravi Sankar, Rx Publications, Tirunelveli.
3. Organic Analytical Chemistry; Theory and Practice, Jag Mohan, Narosa Publishing House, New Delhi.
4. Vogel's Textbook of Quantitative Analysis, Part III, CBS Publishers and Distributors, New Delhi.
5. Practical Pharmaceutical Chemistry, 4th Edition, Part One and Two, A.H. Beckett and J.B. Stenlake, CBS Publishers, New Delhi.
6. Practical Pharmaceutical Chemistry, H. Singh and V.K. Kapoor, Vallabh Prakashan, New Delhi.
7. Indian Pharmacoepia, 1996, Volume I and II.

8. Textbook of Analytical Chemistry: Theory and Practice, R.M. Verma, 3rd Edition, CBS Publishers, New Delhi.
9. Modern Analytical Chemistry, David Harvey, McGraw-Hill Higher Education.
10. Textbook of Pharmaceutical Drug Analysis, 2nd Edition, Ashutosh Kar, New Age International Publishers, Pvt. Ltd., New Delhi.

INDEX